BASEBALL CARDS

Text by
Red Foley

PRICE STERN SLOAN
Los Angeles

Officially licensed by Major League Baseball

Official Licensee

© 1988 MLBPA
© MSA

An MBKA Production

Printed and bound in Hong Kong.

TEAM LEADERS

Year-by-Year Batting Leaders

Home Runs

1961 - Leon Wagner (28)
1962 - Leon Wagner (37)
1963 - Leon Wagner (26)
1964 - Joe Adcock (21)
1965 - Jim Fregosi (15)
1966 - Joe Adcock (18)
1967 - Don Mincher (25)
1968 - Rick Reichardt (21)
1969 - Rick Reichardt (13)
1970 - Jim Fregosi (22)
1971 - Ken McMullen (21)
1972 - Bob Oliver (20)
1973 - Frank Robinson (30)
1974 - Frank Robinson (20)
1975 - Lee Stanton (14)
1976 - Bobby Bonds (10)
1977 - Bobby Bonds (37)
1978 - Don Baylor (34)
1979 - Don Baylor (36)
1980 - Jason Thompson (17)
1981 - Bobby Grich (22)
1982 - Reggie Jackson (39)
1983 - Fred Lynn (22)
1984 - Reggie Jackson (25)
1985 - Reggie Jackson (27)

1986 - Doug DeCinces (26)
1987 - Wally Joyner (34)
1988 - Brian Downing (25)

Runs Batted In

Ken Hunt (84)
Leon Wagner (107)
Leon Wagner (90)
Jim Fregosi (72)
Jim Fregosi (64)
Bobby Knoop (72)
Don Mincher (76)
Rick Reichardt (73)
Rick Reichardt (68)
Alex Johnson (86)
Ken McMullen (68)
Bob Oliver (76)
Frank Robinson (97)
Frank Robinson (63)
Lee Stanton (82)
Bobby Bonds (54)
Bobby Bonds (115)
Don Baylor (99)
Don Baylor (139)
Carney Lansford (80)
Don Baylor (66)
Reggie Jackson (101)
Fred Lynn (74)
Brian Downing (91)
Brian Downing (85)
Reggie Jackson (85)
Wally Joyner (100)
Wally Joyner (117)
Chili Davis (93)

Batting Average

Albie Pearson (.288)
Lee Thomas (.290)
Albie Pearson (.304)
Bob Rodgers (.243)
Jim Fregosi (.277)
Jose Cardenal (.276)
Jim Fregosi (.290)
Rick Reichardt (.255)
Jay Johnstone (.270)
Alex Johnson (.329)
Sandy Alomar (.260)
Vada Pinson (.275)
Frank Robinson (.266)
Mickey Rivers (.285)
Mickey Rivers (.284)
Jerry Remy (.263)
Dave Chalk (.277)
Lyman Bostock (.296)
Brian Downing (.326)
Rod Carew (.331)
Rod Carew (.305)
Rod Carew (.319)
Rod Carew (.339)
Brian Downing (.275)
Rod Carew (.280)

Wally Joyner (.290)
Wally Joyner (.285)
Johnny Ray (.306)

Year-by-Year Pitching Leaders

Wins

1961 - Ken McBride (12)
1962 - Dean Chance (14)
1963 - Dean Chance (13)
        Ken McBride (13)
1964 - Dean Chance (20)
1965 - Dean Chance (15)
1966 - George Brunet (13)
        Jack Sanford(13)
1967 - Rickey Clark (12)
        Jim McGlothlin (12)
        Minnie Rojas (12)
1968 - George Brunet (13)
1969 - Andy Messersmith (16)
1970 - Clyde Wright (22)
1971 - Andy Messersmith (20)
1972 - Nolan Ryan (19)
1973 - Nolan Ryan (21)
1974 - Nolan Ryan (22)
1975 - Ed Figueroa (16)
        Frank Tanana (16)
1976 - Frank Tanana (19)
1977 - Nolan Ryan (19)
1978 - Frank Tanana (18)
1979 - Dave Frost (16)
        Nolan Ryan (16)
1980 - Mark Clear (11)
        Frank Tanana (11)
1981 - Ken Forsch (11)
1982 - Geoff Zahn (18)
1983 - Ken Forsch (11)
        Tommy John (11)
        Bruce Kison (11)
1984 - Mike Witt (15)
1985 - Mike Witt (15)
1986 - Mike Witt (18)
1987 - Mike Witt (16)
1988 - Mike Witt (13)

Strikeouts

Ken McBride (180)
Bo Belinsky (145)
Dean Chance (168)

Dean Chance (207)
Dean Chance (164)
Dean Chance (180)

George Brunet (165)

Jim McGlothlin (135)
Andy Messersmith (211)
Rudy May (164)
Andy Messersmith (179)
Nolan Ryan (329)
Nolan Ryan (383)
Nolan Ryan (367)
Frank Tanana (269)
Nolan Ryan (327)
Nolan Ryan (341)
Nolan Ryan (260)
Nolan Ryan (223)

Frank Tanana (113)

Mike Witt (75)
Bruce Kison (86)
Bruce Kison (83)

Mike Witt (196)
Mike Witt (180)
Mike Witt (208)
Mike Witt (192)
Mike Witt (133)

Earned Run Average

Ken McBride (3.64)
Dean Chance (2.96)
Dean Chance (3.19)

Dean Chance (1.65)
George Brunet (2.56)
Dean Chance (3.08)

Rickey Clark (2.59)

George Brunet (2.86)
Andy Messersmith (2.52)
Clyde Wright (2.83)
Andy Messersmith (2.99)
Clyde Wright (2.99)
Nolan Ryan (2.28)
Nolan Ryan (2.87)
Andy Hassler (2.61)
Frank Tanana (2.62)
Frank Tanana (2.43)
Frank Tanana (2.54)
Frank Tanana (3.65)
Dave Frost (3.57)

Don Aase (4.06)

Ken Forsch (2.88)
Mike Witt (3.51)
Geoff Zahn (3.33)

Geoff Zahn (3.12)
Mike Witt (3.56)
Mike Witt (2.84)
Willie Fraser (3.92)
Mike Witt (4.15)

Owner's Trophy Awards

1962 - Billy Moran
1963 - Jim Fregosi
1964 - Bobby Knoop
1965 - Bobby Knoop
1966 - Bobby Knoop
1967 - Don Mincher
1968 - Bobby Knoop
1969 - Jim Fregosi
1970 - Jim Fregosi
1971 - Ken McMullen
1972 - Bob Oliver, Vada Pinson
1973 - Nolan Ryan
1974 - Nolan Ryan
1975 - Mickey Rivers
1976 - Jerry Remy
1977 - Bobby Bonds
1978 - Don Baylor
1979 - Don Baylor
1980 - Bobby Grich,
        Jason Thompson
1981 - Rick Burleson
1982 - Doug DeCinces
1983 - Bob Boone
1984 - Juan Beniquez,
        Brian Downing
1985 - Donnie Moore
1986 - Mike Witt
1987 - Wally Joyner

Compiled by Bill Haber.

1961

When the American League expanded from eight to 10 teams and adopted a 162-game schedule in 1961, the Los Angeles Angels was the franchise that brought American League baseball to the West Coast. The so-called "experts" predicted Gene Autry's newly minted franchise would have trouble winning 40 games. But manager Bill Rigney fooled a lot of them as his Halos not only finished seventh, ahead of Kansas City and Washington, but won 70 and played .500 ball in their final 90 games.

The cozy confines of LA's Wrigley Field enabled the Angels to have five hitters pole 20 or more homers. Leon Wagner was the leader with 28, while Steve Bilko had 20, Ken Hunt 25, Lee Thomas 24 and Earl Averill 21. Ken McBride, 12-15, was the workhorse of the pitching staff. Eli Grba was 11-13 and Ted Bowsfield 11-8. Ryne Duren (6-12) and Tom Morgan (8-2) handled the bulk of the bullpen duties.

KEN ASPROMONTE
Second Base
Los Angeles Angels

EARL AVERILL
Catcher-Third Base
Los Angeles Angels

JULIO BECQUER
First Base
Los Angeles Angels

STEVE BILKO
First Base
Los Angeles Angels

TED BOWSFIELD
Pitcher
Los Angeles Angels

ROCKY BRIDGES
Shortstop
Los Angeles Angels

JERRY CASALE
Pitcher
Los Angeles Angels

TEX CLEVENGER
Pitcher
Los Angeles Angels

BOB DAVIS Pitcher — Los Angeles Angels

NED GARVER Pitcher — Los Angeles Angels

ELI GRBA Pitcher — Los Angeles Angels

KEN HAMLIN Shortstop — Los Angeles Angels

1961 ROOKIE
KEN HUNT Outfield — Los Angeles Angels

JOHNNY JAMES Pitcher — Los Angeles Angels

TED KLUSZEWSKI First Base — Los Angeles Angels

1961 ROOKIE
GENE LEEK Third Base-Outfield — Los Angeles Angels

1961 ROOKIE
KEN McBRIDE Pitcher — Los Angeles Angels

1961 ROOKIE
RON MOELLER Pitcher — Los Angeles Angels

TOM MORGAN Pitcher — Los Angeles Angels

ALBIE PEARSON Outfield — Los Angeles Angels

DEL RICE Catcher — Los Angeles Angels

ED SADOWSKI Catcher — Los Angeles Angels

1961 ROOKIE
LEROY THOMAS Outfield — Los Angeles Angels

FAYE THRONEBERRY Outfield — Los Angeles Angels

1962

The Angels moved into brand-new Dodger Stadium as tenants of Walter O'Malley and celebrated the shift by finishing a surprising third in the 1962 race. Bill Rigney's club was in the running in September and wound up 10 games behind the winning Yankees. Ken Hunt, a big gun in 1961, was bothered all year by a shoulder separation and Ken McBride, who was 11-3 on July 21, suffered an arm problem that restricted him to only two more starts. Leon Wagner was the club's home run leader with 37 and 107 RBIs. Lee Thomas hit 26 and drove home 104. Rookie righthander Dean Chance was the Angels' top pitcher with 14 wins. Bo Belinsky, who no-hit Boston in May, finished 10-11. McBride was 11-5 and Ted Bowsfield 9-8.

JIM
DONOHUE
L. A. ANGELS P

RYNE
DUREN
L. A. ANGELS P

ART
FOWLER
L. A. ANGELS P

1962 ROOKIE

JIM
FREGOSI
L. A. ANGELS SS

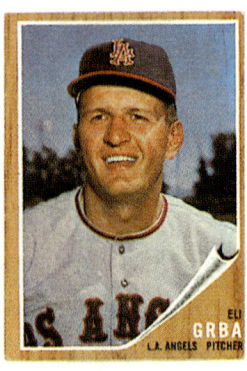

ELI
GRBA
L. A. ANGELS PITCHER

KEN L.
HUNT
L. A. ANGELS OUTFIELD

JOE
KOPPE
L. A. ANGELS SS

KEN
McBRIDE
L. A. ANGELS P

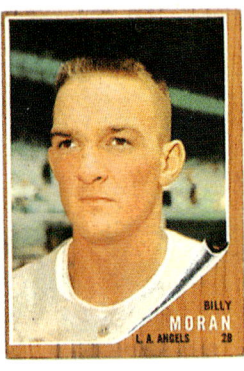

BILLY
MORAN
L. A. ANGELS 2B

TOM
MORGAN
L. A. ANGELS PITCHER

ALBIE
PEARSON
L. A. ANGELS OF

BILL
RIGNEY
L. A. ANGELS MGR.

1962 ROOKIE

BOB
RODGERS
L. A. ANGELS C

ED
SADOWSKI
L. A. ANGELS C

JACK
SPRING
L. A. ANGELS P

GEORGE
THOMAS
L. A. ANGELS OF-3B

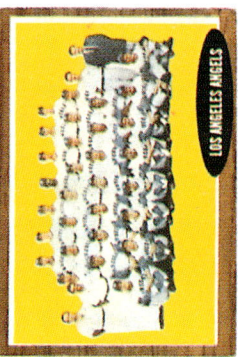

≡1963≡

After their spectacular season in 1962, the Angels experienced a flop to ninth place in 1963. Albie Pearson's .304 average was highest among the regulars while Leon Wagner's 26 homers and 90 RBIs led those categories. Shortstop Jim Fregosi batted .287 and second baseman Billy Moran batted .275. The pitching was a problem throughout the season. Ken McBride went 13-12 while Dean Chance finished 13-18. Dan Osinski was 8-8, Don Lee 8-11. Bo Belinsky, the colorful southpaw, ended up with a 2-9 record. Belinsky, however, gained considerable notoriety for his after-dark exploits with the Broadway and Hollywood crowd, particularly movie actress Mamie Van Doren and famed columnist Walter Winchell.

BO
BELINSKY
L. A. ANGELS   PITCHER

LEO
BURKE
L. A. ANGELS   INF.

DEAN
CHANCE
L. A. ANGELS   P.

JACKE
DAVIS
L. A. ANGELS   OF

RYNE
DUREN
L. A. ANGELS   PITCHER

ART
FOWLER
LOS ANGELES ANGELS   P

JIM
FREGOSI
LOS ANGELES ANGELS   SS

ELI
GRBA
L. A. ANGELS   PITCHER

KEN
HUNT
L. A. ANGELS   OF

JOE
KOPPE
LOS ANGELES ANGELS   SS

DON
LEE
LOS ANGELES ANGELS   P

KEN
McBRIDE
LOS ANGELES ANGELS   P

RON
MOELLER
L. A. ANGELS   PITCHER

BILLY
MORAN
L. A. ANGELS   2B

TOM
MORGAN
LOS ANGELES ANGELS   P

DAN
OSINSKI
L. A. ANGELS   PITCHER

ALBIE
PEARSON
LOS ANGELES ANGELS OF

BILL
RIGNEY
L. A. ANGELS MGR

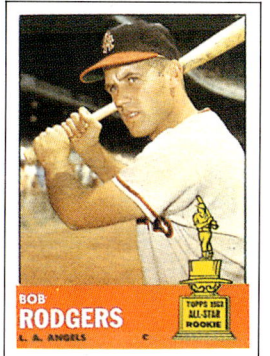

BOB
RODGERS
L. A. ANGELS C

TOPPS 1962
ALL-STAR
ROOKIE

BOB
SADOWSKI
L. A. ANGELS INF

ED
SADOWSKI
L. A. ANGELS C

TOM
SATRIANO
L. A. ANGELS 3B

JACK
SPRING
L. A. ANGELS PITCHER

GEORGE
THOMAS
L. A. ANGELS OF

LEE
THOMAS
L. A. ANGELS OF-1B

FELIX
TORRES
LOS ANGELES ANGELS 3B

BOB
TURLEY
L. A. ANGELS P

LEON
WAGNER
L. A. ANGELS OF

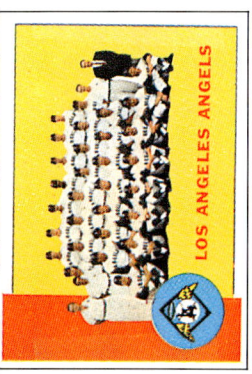

LOS ANGELES ANGELS

1964

Dean Chance, winning 20 while losing nine, was the Cy Young Award winner and his 1.65 earned run average led the league as the rebounding Angels advanced to fifth place in 1964. Complementing Chance on the pitching staff were Fred Newman, 13-10, Bo Belinsky, 9-8, Barry Latman, 6-10, and Bob Lee, 6-5. Outfielder Jimmy Piersall batted .314 and Willie Smith .301. Joe Adcock led the Halos in homers with 21. Jim Fregosi hit 18 and paced his mates in RBIs with 72. During the season outfielder Rick Reichardt, a $200,000 bonus baby, was signed and got into 11 games. It was manager Bill Rigney's pitching that kept the Angels solvent. They not only fashioned a 2.91 ERA but authored 28 shutouts, the most in the majors since 1909.

ANGELS

BO BELINSKY   pitcher

ANGELS

DEAN CHANCE   pitcher

ANGELS

CHARLIE DEES   1st base

ANGELS

BOB DULIBA   pitcher

ANGELS

HANK FOILES   catcher

ANGELS

ART FOWLER   pitcher

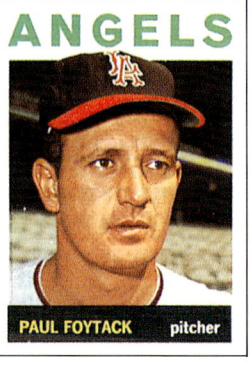

ANGELS

PAUL FOYTACK   pitcher

ANGELS

JIM FREGOSI   shortstop

ANGELS

ED KIRKPATRICK   c-of

ANGELS

JOE KOPPE   shortstop

ANGELS

BARRY LATMAN   pitcher

ANGELS

DON LEE   pitcher

ANGELS

KEN McBRIDE   pitcher

ANGELS

BILLY MORAN   2b-3b

ANGELS

MEL NELSON   pitcher

ANGELS

FRED NEWMAN   pitcher

ANGELS

DAN OSINSKI   pitcher

ANGELS

ALBIE PEARSON   outfield

ANGELS

BOB PERRY   outfield

ANGELS

JIM PIERSALL   outfield

ANGELS

BILL RIGNEY   manager

ANGELS

BOB RODGERS   catcher

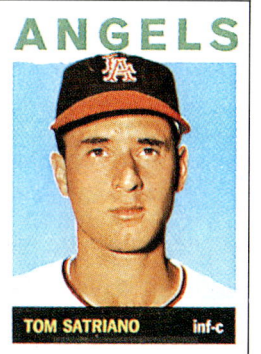

ANGELS

TOM SATRIANO   inf-c

ANGELS

JACK SPRING   pitcher

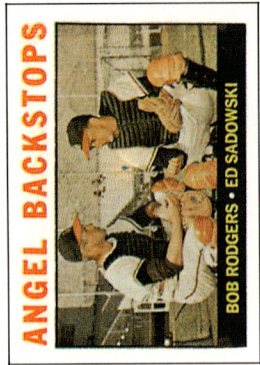

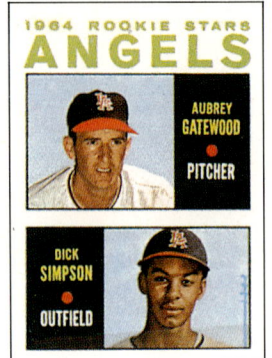

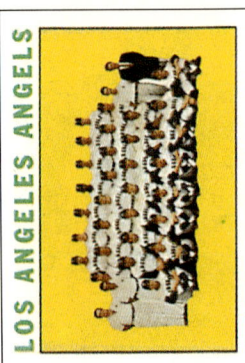

1965

In what was their final season as tenants at Dodger Stadium, the 1965 Angels finished a disappointing seventh, drawing less than 600,000 at home. The club didn't own a hitter over .280 as Albie Pearson's .278 was tops. Jim Fregosi batted .277 and his 15 homers and 64 RBIs were club highs. Bobby Knoop hit .269 and Willie Smith, hitting .261, had 14 homers, the same as Joe Adcock. Dean Chance, with 15, led the Angels in victories among the moundsmen. Marcelino Lopez went 14-13 and Fred Newman 14-16. George Brunet and Bob Lee each accounted for nine victories while lefthander Rudy May finished with a 4-9 record.

PITCHER
GEORGE BRUNET

PITCHER
DEAN CHANCE

OUTFIELD
GINO CIMOLI

OUTFIELD
LOU CLINTON

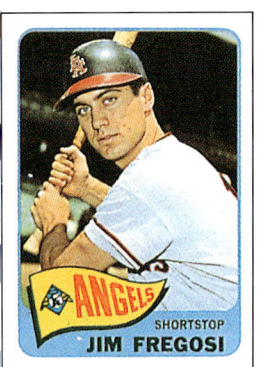

SHORTSTOP
JIM FREGOSI

PITCHER
AUBREY GATEWOOD

3B-SS
JULIO GOTAY

OUTFIELD
ED KIRKPATRICK

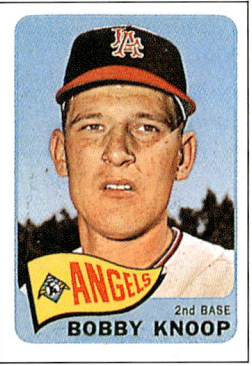

2nd BASE
BOBBY KNOOP

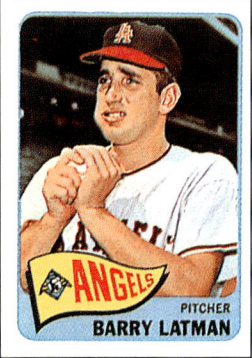

PITCHER
BARRY LATMAN

PITCHER
BOB LEE

PITCHER
DON LEE

PITCHER
BOBBY LOCKE

PITCHER
KEN McBRIDE

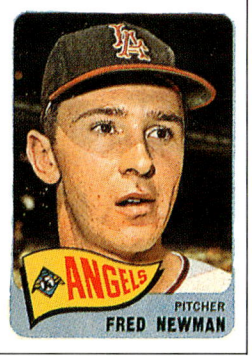

PITCHER
FRED NEWMAN

OUTFIELD
ALBIE PEARSON

RON PICHE
PITCHER

JIM PIERSALL
OUTFIELD

VIC POWER
1B-INF

BILL RIGNEY
MANAGER

BOB RODGERS
CATCHER

TOM SATRIANO
INF-CATCHER

WILLIE SMITH
OUTFIELD

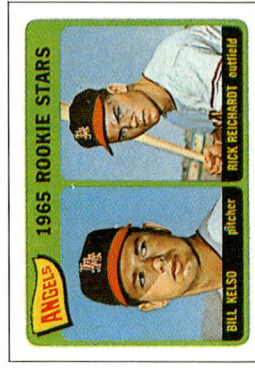

1965 ROOKIE STARS
RICK REICHARDT outfield
BILL KELSO pitcher
ANGELS

1965 ROOKIE STARS
DICK SIMPSON outfield
JOSE CARDENAL outfield
ANGELS

1965 ROOKIE STARS
PAT ROGAN pitcher
TOM EGAN catcher-3 b
ANGELS

1965 ROOKIE STARS
JACK WARNER outfield
PAUL SCHAAL 3rd base
ANGELS

ANGELS 1965 ROOKIE STARS
MARCELINO LOPEZ PITCHER
RUDY MAY PITCHER
PHIL ROOF CATCHER

ANGELS
5TH PLACE · AMERICAN LEAGUE

1966

The Angels' move to a new home in Anaheim was a fiscal success but something of an artistic failure and the club, in contention until August, wound up in sixth place in 1966. Injuries hampered the club, particularly those to Rick Reichardt, Fred Newman and Albie Pearson. Reichardt, limited to 89 games, batted .288 and hit 16 homers and had 44 RBIs when a kidney ailment that required surgery ended his season in late July. A sore shoulder restricted Newman to a mere four wins, while a spinal problem, suffered in spring training, eventually earned Pearson his release. Joe Adcock hit 18 homers and Bobby Knoop 17. Despite batting .232, Knoop's 72 RBIs were high for the team. Dean Chance won 17 and lost 17. Marcy Lopez won seven and lost 14. George Brunet was 8-8 while veterans Jack Sanford and Lou Burdette contributed. Sanford was 13-7 and Burdette, strictly in relief, was 7-2.

GEORGE BRUNET   pitcher

LOU BURDETTE   pitcher

JOSE CARDENAL   outfield

DEAN CHANCE   pitcher

DICK EGAN   pitcher

TOM EGAN   catcher

JIM FREGOSI   shortstop

AUBREY GATEWOOD   pitcher

ED KIRKPATRICK — outfield

BOBBY KNOOP — 2b

BOB LEE — pitcher

MARCELINO LOPEZ — pitcher

FRANK MALZONE — 3rd base

FRED NEWMAN — pitcher

ALBIE PEARSON — outfield

JIMMY PIERSALL — outfield

VIC POWER — 1b-inf

MERRITT RANEW — catcher

RICK REICHARDT — outfield

BILL RIGNEY — manager

BOB RODGERS — catcher

JACK SANFORD — pitcher

TOM SATRIANO — catcher

PAUL SCHAAL — 3rd base

WILLIE SMITH   outfield

AL SPANGLER   outfield

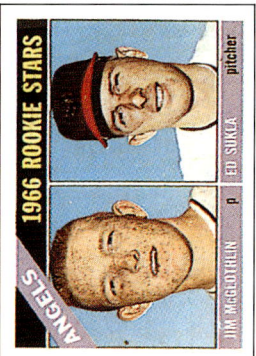

1966 ROOKIE STARS   ED SUKLA   pitcher   JIM McGLOTHLIN   p   ANGELS

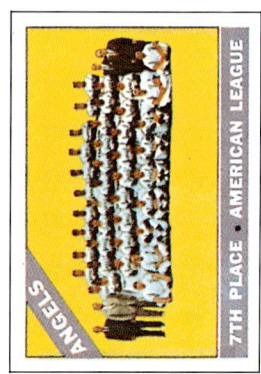

7TH PLACE • AMERICAN LEAGUE   ANGELS

≡1967≡

The 1967 season was one of contrasts for the Angels and veteran manager Bill Rigney. They got off to a horrendous start yet by mid-August were 1½ games away from the top spot, eventually finishing fifth, 7½ lengths behind. When performing at home the Angels were super, winning 53 and losing 30. On the road, however, they were terrible, losing 47 of 78.

Jim Fregosi led the offense with a .290 average while the newly acquired Don Mincher and Jimmie Hall contributed nicely. Mincher hit 25 homers and had 76 RBIs and Hall hit 16 and drove in 55. Bonus baby Rick Reichardt, slow to recover from kidney surgery, had 17 homers and 69 RBIs. Pitching was a season-long problem. Dean Chance was dealt to Minnesota in the spring and Marcy Lopez to Baltimore in mid-season. Fred Newman, pitching only six innings, indicated he hadn't recovered from arm surgery. Youngster Jim McGlothlin (12-8) and Rick Clark (12-11) picked up some slack. George Brunet was 11-19 and Minnie Rojas, mostly from the 'pen, finished 12-9.

GEORGE BRUNET • P   ANGELS

LOU BURDETTE • PITCHER   ANGELS

JOSE CARDENAL • OF   ANGELS

PETE CIMINO PITCHER   ANGELS

JIM COATES • PITCHER

ANGELS

TOM EGAN • CATCHER

ANGELS

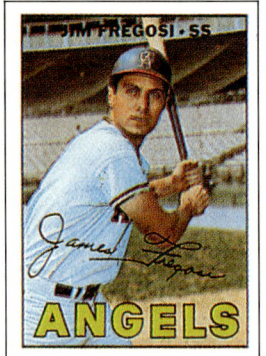

JIM FREGOSI • SS

ANGELS

LEN GABRIELSON • OF

ANGELS

JIMMIE HALL • OUTFIELD

ANGELS

JAY JOHNSTONE • OF

ANGELS

ED KIRKPATRICK • OF

ANGELS

BOBBY KNOOP • 2B

ANGELS

MARCELINO LOPEZ • P

ANGELS

ORLANDO McFARLANE • C

ANGELS

JIM McGLOTHLIN PITCHER

ANGELS

DON MINCHER • 1B

ANGELS

BUBBA MORTON OUTFIELD

ANGELS

FRED NEWMAN • PITCHER

ANGELS

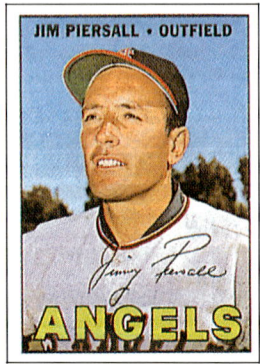

JIM PIERSALL • OUTFIELD

ANGELS

RICK REICHARDT OUTFIELD

ANGELS

BILL RIGNEY • MGR.

ANGELS

BOB RODGERS • CATCHER

ANGELS

MINNIE ROJAS PITCHER

ANGELS

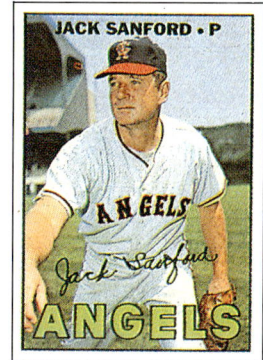

JACK SANFORD • P

ANGELS

TOM SATRIANO • C-3B

ANGELS

PAUL SCHAAL 3B

ANGELS

NICK WILLHITE • P

ANGELS

ANGELS 1967 ROOKIE STARS

DON WALLACE • INF

BILL KELSO • P

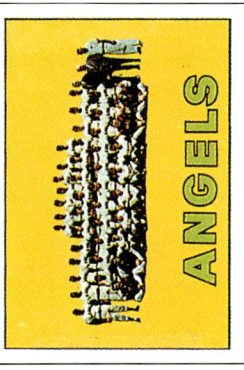

ANGELS

1968

A season the Angels looked toward with great optimism turned out to be something entirely different as the club, never prominent in the standings, landed in eighth place in 1968. The troubles began early, such as the second game of the season, when slugger Don Mincher was beaned by Cleveland fireballer Sam McDowell. He never fully recovered and wound up hitting .236 with 13 homers and 48 RBIs. A bright spot was Tom Satriano. The catcher hit .253 and handled the pitchers well. Rookie pitchers Tom Murphy and Andy Messersmith comported themselves nicely. Murphy was 5-6 in 15 starts and Messersmith, as a starter and reliever, was 4-2. George Brunet was 13-17, Clyde Wright 10-6 and Jim McGlothlin 10-15. Reliever Minnie Rojas, missing most of the second half with ailments, had only four wins and six saves.

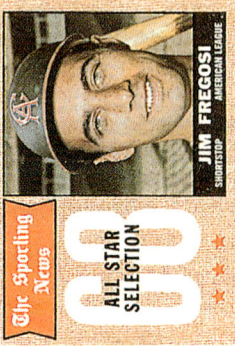
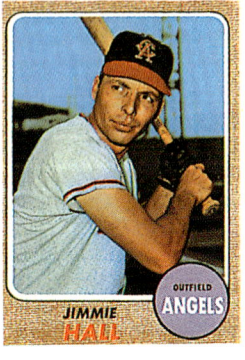

WOODY
HELD
INF-OF
ANGELS

CHUCK
HINTON
OF-1B
ANGELS

JAY
JOHNSTONE
OUTFIELD
ANGELS

ED
KIRKPATRICK
OF-CATCHER
ANGELS

BOBBY
KNOOP
2nd BASE
ANGELS

BOBBY
LOCKE
PITCHER
ANGELS

JIM
McGLOTHLIN
PITCHER
ANGELS

DON
MINCHER
1st BASE
ANGELS

BUBBA
MORTON
OUTFIELD
ANGELS

RICK
REICHARDT
OUTFIELD
ANGELS

ROGER
REPOZ
OUTFIELD
ANGELS

BILL
RIGNEY
MANAGER
ANGELS

BOB
RODGERS
CATCHER
ANGELS

MINNIE
ROJAS
PITCHER
ANGELS

TOM
SATRIANO
CATCHER -3B
ANGELS

PAUL
SCHAAL
3rd BASE
ANGELS

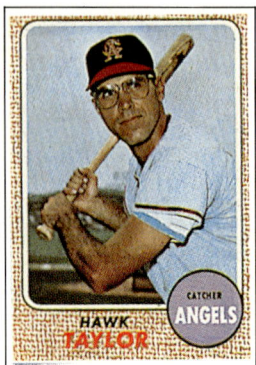
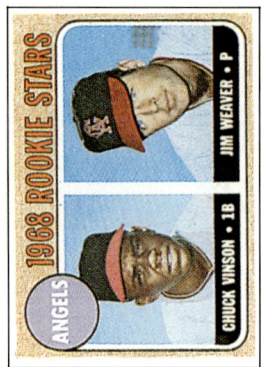

1969

The American League expanded to a dozen clubs in 1969 as baseball adopted the two-division system. The Angels did finish third in the West, whereas under the old system they would have been nestled in eighth place. In late May, with the club at the bottom, Bill Rigney was canned as manager. Harold (Lefty) Phillips replaced him and the Angels played an uninspired 60-63 under his guidance. Jim Fregosi batted .260 and Rick Reichardt hit 13 home runs and had 68 RBIs, both club highs for the year. Jay Johnstone, promoted after Phillips' hiring, batted .270 and drove in 59 runs. Andy Messersmith's 16 wins topped the staff. Rudy May was 10-13 and Tom Murphy 10-16. Jim McGlothlin fell off to 8-16 while bullpenner Ken Tatum won seven and saved 22.

  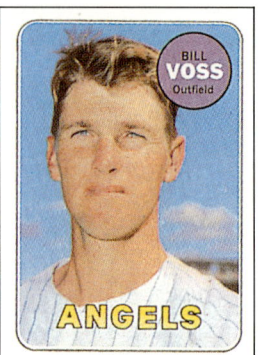 

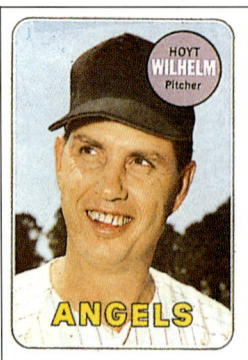  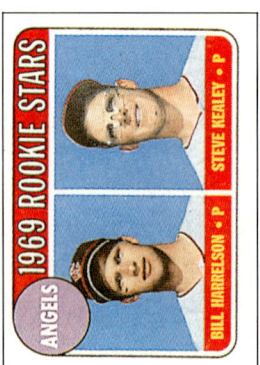

1970

Following several seasons in which they weren't a factor in the American League standings, the 1970 Angels' edition landed in third place in the West. Controversial outfielder Alex Johnson led the league in batting with a .329 average. He bested Boston's Carl Yastrzemski by .0003 in the final arithmetic.

Jim Fregosi hit .278 with 22 homers and Jim Spencer hit .278 with 68 RBIs. Only three games behind the Twins in early September, a series of injuries took the Angels out of the race. Clyde Wright, who won only one game in 1969, rebounded for a 22-12 season in 1970. Tom Murphy was 16-13 and Andy Messersmith, bothered by injuries, was 11-10. Reliever Ken Tatum won seven as did Rudy May, whose value was minimized by his 13 defeats.

Sandy Alomar 2ND BASE

Jose Azcue CATCHER

Rickey Clark PITCHER

Paul Doyle PITCHER

Tom Egan CATCHER

Eddie Fisher PITCHER

Jack Fisher PITCHER

Jim Fregosi SHORTSTOP

Jim Hicks OUTFIELD

Jay Johnstone OUTFIELD

Rudy May PITCHER

Jim McGlothlin PITCHER

A. Messersmith PITCHER

Tom Murphy PITCHER

Lefty Phillips MANAGER

Rich Reichardt OUTFIELD

Roger Repoz | OUTFIELD

Aurelio Rodriguez | 3RD BASE

Chico Ruiz | INFIELD

Jim Spencer | 1ST BASE

Ken Tatum | PITCHER

Bill Voss | OUTFIELD

Clyde Wright | PITCHER

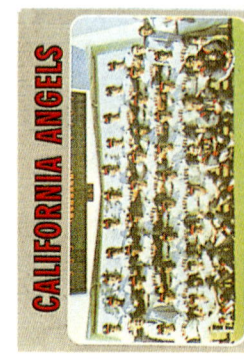

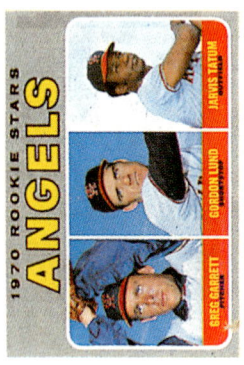

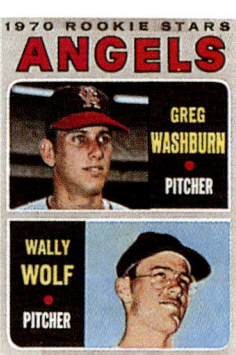

1971

Predicted by many to be Western Division titlists in 1971, the unpredictable Angels, their season peppered by problems with defending batting champion Alex Johnson, finished fourth, 25½ lengths behind Oakland. Johnson was dealt to Cleveland after playing only 65 games, hitting a mere .260 and following a series of misadventures in which he claimed "emotional stress." Jim Fregosi, bothered by a foot problem, hit only .233. Jim Spencer hit 18 homers and had 59 RBIs. Sandy Alomar batted .260 and was solid at second base. Mickey Rivers, a newcomer, batted .265. Andy Messersmith won 20 games and Clyde Wright 16. Rudy May finished 11-12, while Eddie Fisher was 10-8. Dave LaRoche, a reliever, was 5-1 with nine saves.

ANGELS · shortstop
jim fregosi

ANGELS   outfield
tony gonzalez

ANGELS   pitcher
ray jarvis

ANGELS   outfield
alex johnson

ANGELS   pitcher
steve kealey

ANGELS   pitcher
dave laroche

ANGELS   pitcher
fred lasher
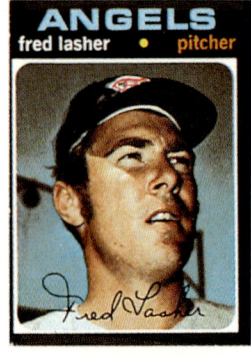

ANGELS   pitcher
jim maloney

ANGELS · pitcher
rudy may
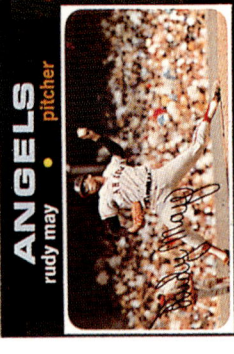

ANGELS   3rd base
ken mc mullen

ANGELS   p
andy messersmith

ANGELS   catcher
gerry moses

ANGELS · pitcher
tom murphy

ANGELS · infield
syd o'brien

ANGELS   manager
lefty phillips

ANGELS   pitcher
mel queen

ANGELS
roger repoz • outfield

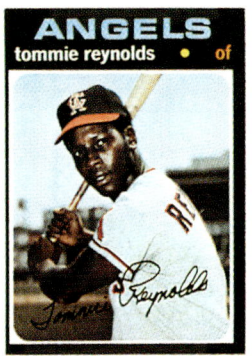

ANGELS
tommie reynolds • of

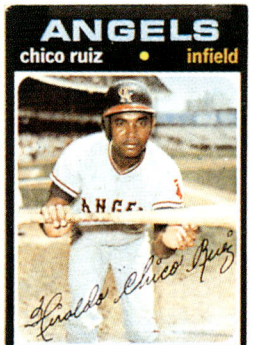

ANGELS
chico ruiz • infield

ANGELS
jim spencer • 1st base

ANGELS
john stephenson • catcher

ANGELS
clyde wright • pitcher

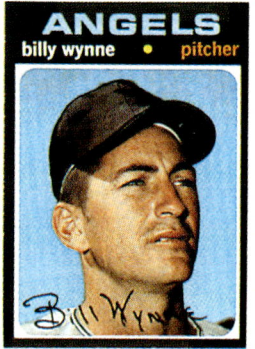

ANGELS
billy wynne • pitcher

1971 ROOKIE STARS
ANGELS
lloyd allen • pitcher
winston llenas • third base

ANGELS

1972

Despite dropping another notch in the standings to fifth place, the 1972 Angels produced a harmony and brand of baseball that augured well for the future. A cause for much of the change was the addition of Nolan Ryan from the Mets. The hard-throwing righthander not only won 19 games but led the league with 329 strikeouts while pitching 284 innings. Ryan was abetted by 18-game-winner Clyde Wright and lefty Rudy May who won a dozen.

Manager Del Rice was not so fortunate regarding the club's offense. Vada Pinson, at .275, had the highest average for a regular. Ken McMullen batted .269. Leroy Stanton, who accompanied Ryan from New York, had a dozen home runs while Bob Oliver, traded from Kansas City, popped 19 homers and drove home 70 runs for the Angels.

LLOYD ALLEN

SANDY ALOMAR

KEN BERRY

LEO CARDENAS

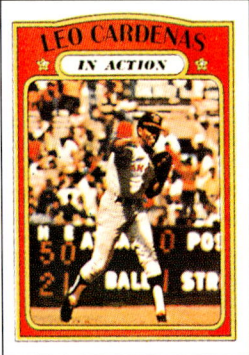
LEO CARDENAS IN ACTION

RICKEY CLARK

BILLY COWAN

PAUL DOYLE

EDDIE FISHER

ALAN FOSTER

JIM FREGOSI

RUDY MAY

KEN McMULLEN

ANDY MESSERSMITH

TOM MURPHY

SYD O'BRIEN

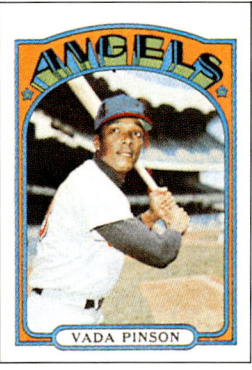

VADA PINSON

MEL QUEEN

ROGER REPOZ

ARCHIE REYNOLDS

DEL RICE

MICKEY RIVERS

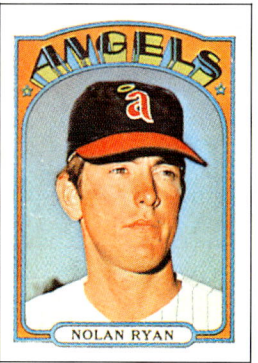

NOLAN RYAN

JIM SPENCER

JEFF TORBORG

CLYDE WRIGHT

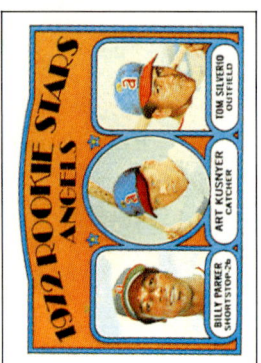
1972 ROOKIE STARS
ANGELS

TOM SILVERIO OUTFIELD

ART KUSNYER CATCHER

BILLY PARKER SHORTSTOP-2b

ANGELS

1973

Nolan Ryan's victories, two no-hitters and record-setting 383 strikeouts weren't sufficient to keep the Angels from finishing fourth in the Western Division in 1973. Bobby Winkles, a successful collegiate coach at Arizona State University, became the Halos' skipper in 1973 and, in addition to Ryan, got a banner season from veteran outfielder Frank Robinson and a rebounding Bill Singer. Robby hit .266 and banged 30 homers while driving in 97 runs. Singer, who'd lost 33 games the previous two years, regained his form and posted a 20-14 record. Clyde Wright won 11 but dropped 19. Assisting Robinson at the plate was Bob Oliver, who had 18 home runs and 89 RBIs. Bobby Valentine, batting .302, had his season cut short by a broken leg on May 17.

LLOYD
ALLEN
CALIFORNIA ANGELS   PITCHER

SANDY
ALOMAR
CALIFORNIA ANGELS   2nd BASE

STEVE
BARBER
CALIFORNIA ANGELS   PITCHER

KEN
BERRY
CALIFORNIA ANGELS   OUTFIELD

LEO
CARDENAS
CALIFORNIA ANGELS   SHORTSTOP

RICK
CLARK
CALIFORNIA ANGELS   PITCHER

ALAN
FOSTER
CALIFORNIA ANGELS   PITCHER

BILLY
GRABARKEWITZ
CALIFORNIA ANGELS   3rd BASE

JACK
HIATT
CALIFORNIA ANGELS   CATCHER

RUDY
MAY
CALIFORNIA ANGELS   PITCHER

BOB
OLIVER
CALIFORNIA ANGELS   1st BASE

BILLY
PARKER
CALIFORNIA ANGELS   2nd BASE

VADA
PINSON
CALIFORNIA ANGELS   OUTFIELD

MICKEY
RIVERS
CALIFORNIA ANGELS   OUTFIELD

OUTFIELD

FRANK
ROBINSON
CALIFORNIA ANGELS

DON
ROSE
CALIFORNIA ANGELS   PITCHER

NOLAN
RYAN
CALIFORNIA ANGELS   PITCHER

BILL
SINGER
CALIFORNIA ANGELS   PITCHER

JIM
SPENCER
CALIFORNIA ANGELS   1st BASE

LEROY
STANTON
CALIFORNIA ANGELS   OUTFIELD

MIKE
STRAHLER
CALIFORNIA ANGELS   PITCHER

JEFF
TORBORG
CALIFORNIA ANGELS   'CATCHER

BOBBY
VALENTINE
CALIFORNIA ANGELS   OUTFIELD

CLYDE
WRIGHT
CALIFORNIA ANGELS   PITCHER

1974

It was another winning season for Nolan Ryan but considerably less for his Angels who, for the first time in their checkered history, toppled into the Western Division cellar in 1974. While Ryan was winning 22 games, tossing his third career no-hitter and exceeding 300 strikeouts for the third straight year, the Angels were firing Bobby Winkles and replacing him with Dick Williams.

In addition a series of injuries put at least one Angels player on the disabled list from opening day through closing. Aiding Ryan were youngsters Frank Tanana, 14-19, and Andy Hassler, 7-11. Sore-armed Bill Singer won seven. Rookie infielder Dave Chalk batted .252 and Mickey Rivers hit .285 with 30 stolen bases. Prior to his late-season waiver to Cleveland, where he would become baseball's first black manager, Frank Robinson hit 20 homers and had 63 runs batted in.

CALIFORNIA 2nd BASE
SANDY ALOMAR ANGELS

CALIFORNIA OUTFIELD
OLLIE BROWN ANGELS

CALIFORNIA 2nd BASE
DENNY DOYLE ANGELS

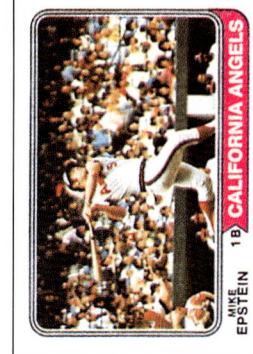

CALIFORNIA ANGELS
MIKE EPSTEIN 1B

CALIFORNIA PITCHER
RICH HAND ANGELS

CALIFORNIA OUTFIELD
JOE LAHOUD ANGELS

CALIFORNIA PITCHER
DICK LANGE ANGELS

CALIFORNIA 2B-3B
WINSTON LLENAS ANGELS

CALIFORNIA PITCHER
SKIP LOCKWOOD ANGELS

CALIFORNIA PITCHER
RUDY MAY ANGELS

CALIFORNIA 1B-OF
TOM McCRAW ANGELS

CALIFORNIA SHORTSTOP
RUDY MEOLI ANGELS

CALIFORNIA PITCHER
AURELIO MONTEAGUDO ANGELS

CALIFORNIA 1B-3B
BOB OLIVER ANGELS

CALIFORNIA ANGELS
VADA PINSON OF

CALIFORNIA OUTFIELD
MICKEY RIVERS ANGELS

CALIFORNIA DH—OF
FRANK ROBINSON
ANGELS

CALIFORNIA CATCHER
ELLIE RODRIGUEZ
ANGELS

CALIFORNIA PITCHER
NOLAN RYAN
ANGELS

CALIFORNIA CATCHER
CHARLIE SANDS
ANGELS

CALIFORNIA OUTFIELD
RICHIE SCHEINBLUM
ANGELS

CALIFORNIA PITCHER
DAVE SELLS
ANGELS

CALIFORNIA PITCHER
BILL SINGER
ANGELS

CALIFORNIA OUTFIELD
LEROY STANTON
ANGELS

CALIFORNIA CATCHER
RICK STELMASZEK
ANGELS

CALIFORNIA SHORTSTOP
BOBBY VALENTINE
ANGELS

CALIFORNIA MANAGER
• COACHES •
John Roseboro   Tom Morgan   Jimmie Reese   Salty Parker
BOBBY WINKLES
ANGELS

CALIFORNIA ANGELS

1975

The Angels, hoping to steal a pennant, couldn't even escape from the Western Division basement in 1975. The club swiped 220 bases—the most by any club in 59 years—and still finished 25½ games behind division-leading Oakland. Nolan Ryan, a 10-game winner in June and author of another no-hitter, was beset by physical problems and wound up 14-12 and having an elbow operation. Arm ailments reduced Bill Singer to 7-15. Young Frank Tanana, 16-9 with a 2.63 ERA and 269 strikeouts, took up some slack as did 16-game-winning Ed Figueroa. The lack of longball power virtually destroyed Dick Williams' managerial efforts. The Halos hit only 55 homers and Leroy Stanton, with 14, was the club leader.

BRUCE BOCHTE

DAVE CHALK

CHUCK DOBSON

JOHN DOHERTY

DENNY DOYLE

TOM EGAN

ED FIGUEROA

ANDY HASSLER

BOBBY HEISE

JOE LAHOUD

DICK LANGE

WINSTON LLENAS

SKIP LOCKWOOD

RUDY MEOLI

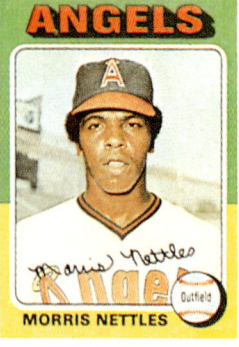
MORRIS NETTLES

ORLANDO PENA

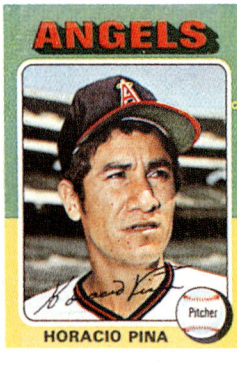
HORACIO PINA

MICKEY RIVERS

ELLIE RODRIGUEZ

RYAN FANS 300—3rd YEAR IN ROW

NOLAN RYAN

KEN SANDERS

CHARLIE SANDS

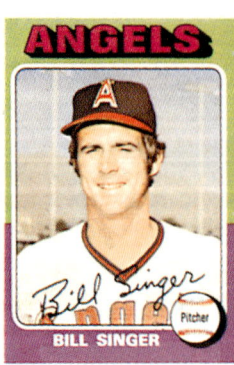
BILL SINGER

LEROY STANTON

FRANK TANANA

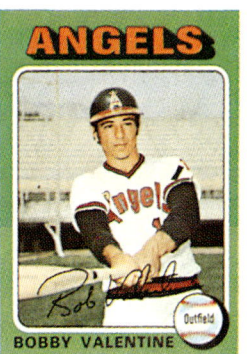
BOBBY VALENTINE

ANGELS

1976

Another managerial switch, 17 wins from Nolan Ryan, plus his fourth 300 strikeout season, all added up to the Angels advancing from the cellar to fourth place in 1976. Dick Williams was fired July 23 and coach Norm Sherry took over. A finger injury to Bobby Bonds in April restricted his season and he hit only 10 homers which, incidentally, was sufficient to lead the club. Second baseman Jerry Remy was a pleasant surprise with his .263 average. Bill Melton, a former White Sox slugger, hit a disappointing six homers and Leroy Stanton finished with a .190 batting average. Along with Ryan, the Angels got class pitching from Frank Tanana, 19-10. Former collegian Paul Hartzell, going from the bullpen to starter, finished 7-4. Lefty Andy Hassler ended up 0-6.

BOB ALLIETTA
CATCHER ANGELS

JOHN BALAZ
OUTFIELD ANGELS

BRUCE BOCHTE
OUTFIELD ANGELS

DEC. 11 SPORTS EXTRA 1975
YANKEES TRADE BONDS TO ANGELS
OUTFIELD BOBBY BONDS

JIM BREWER
PITCHER **ANGELS**

DAVE CHALK
THIRD BASE **ANGELS**

DAVE COLLINS
OUTFIELD **ANGELS**

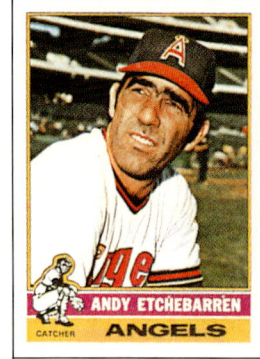

ANDY ETCHEBARREN
CATCHER **ANGELS**

ED FIGUEROA
PITCHER **ANGELS**

ANDY HASSLER
PITCHER **ANGELS**

DON KIRKWOOD
PITCHER **ANGELS**

JOE LAHOUD
DES. HITTER **ANGELS**

DICK LANGE
PITCHER **ANGELS**

DEC. 11 SPORTS EXTRA 1975
ANGELS GET SLUGGER
MELTON OF CHISOX
THIRD BASE **BILL MELTON**

RUDY MEOLI
SECOND BASE **ANGELS**

MIKE MILEY
SHORTSTOP **ANGELS**

MORRIS NETTLES
OUTFIELD **ANGELS**

JERRY REMY
SECOND BASE **ANGELS**

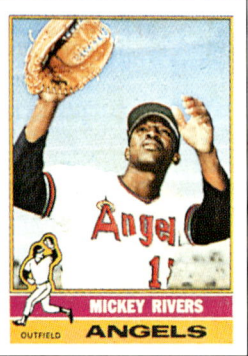

MICKEY RIVERS
OUTFIELD **ANGELS**

ELLIE RODRIGUEZ
CATCHER **ANGELS**

NOLAN RYAN
PITCHER ANGELS

MICKEY SCOTT
PITCHER ANGELS

BILL SINGER
PITCHER ANGELS

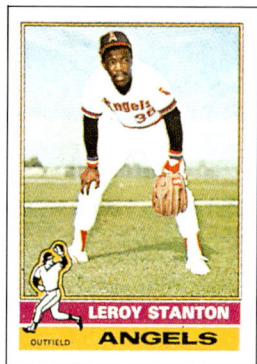

LEROY STANTON
OUTFIELD ANGELS

FRANK TANANA
PITCHER ANGELS

CALIFORNIA ANGELS

1977

The advent of free agency late in 1976 prompted Angels owner Gene Autry to open his saddlebags as the onetime cowboy film star signed a trio for an estimated $8 million. Autry's lavish spending and general manager Harry Dalton's deals had people picking the Halos to win it all in 1977.

Don Baylor, Bobby Grich and Joe Rudi, the free agents signed by Autry, were each hurt by injuries. Baylor, playing hurt, hit 25 homers. Bobby Bonds hammered 30 homers and stole 41 bases. The club's slow start resulted in Norm Sherry's firing and Dave Garcia's promotion to manager. Frank Tanana had 15 wins and his 2.54 ERA was the lowest in the league. Nolan Ryan was 19-16 and again led in strikeouts with 341. Ken Brett won seven games and reliever Dave LaRoche won six and saved 13 after coming to the Angels from Cleveland.

ANGELS 1B-OF
DON BAYLOR

ANGELS 1B-OF
BRUCE BOCHTE

ANGELS OUTFIELD
BOBBY BONDS
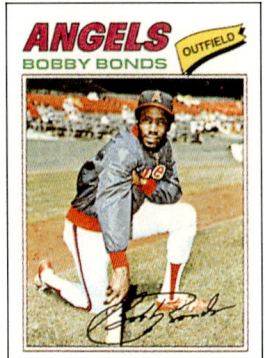

ANGELS 1B-OF
DAN BRIGGS
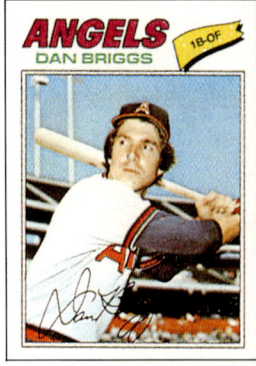

ANGELS SS-3B
DAVE CHALK

ANGELS PITCHER
DICK DRAGO
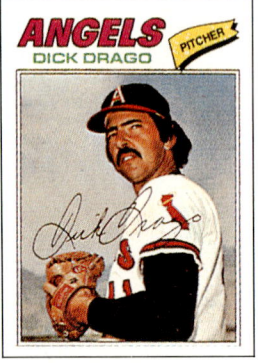

ANGELS CATCHER
ANDY ETCHEBARREN
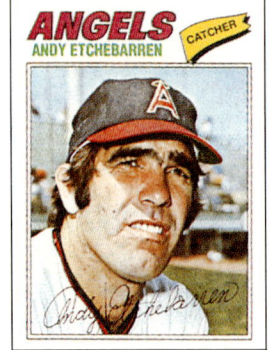

ANGELS 2nd BASE
BOB GRICH
A.L. ALL-STARS

ANGELS SS-2B
MARIO GUERRERO

ANGELS PITCHER
PAUL HARTZELL

ANGELS CATCHER
TERRY HUMPHREY

ANGELS 3rd BASE
RON JACKSON

ANGELS OUTFIELD
BOB JONES

ANGELS PITCHER
DON KIRKWOOD

ANGELS 1B-3B
BILL MELTON

ANGELS SHORTSTOP
MIKE MILEY

ANGELS PITCHER
SID MONGE

ANGELS SHORTSTOP
ORLANDO RAMIREZ

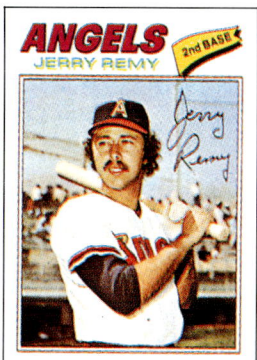

ANGELS 2nd BASE
JERRY REMY

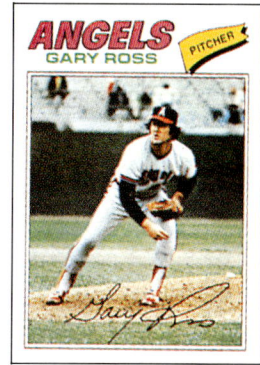

ANGELS PITCHER
GARY ROSS

ANGELS 1B - OF
JOE RUDI

RECORD BREAKER
1978 NOLAN RYAN • ANGELS
MOST SEASONS,
300-OR-MORE STRIKEOUTS

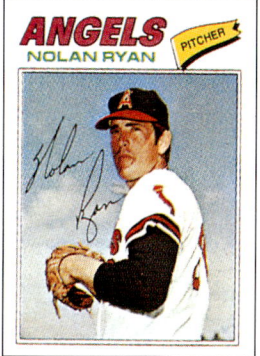

ANGELS PITCHER
NOLAN RYAN

ANGELS PITCHER
MICKEY SCOTT

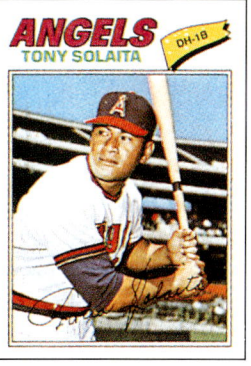

ANGELS DH-1B
TONY SOLAITA

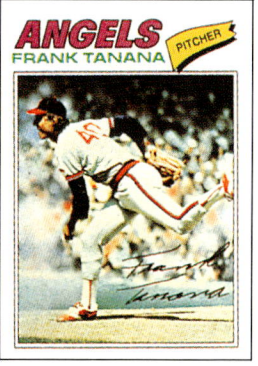

ANGELS PITCHER
FRANK TANANA

ANGELS OUTFIELD
RUSTY TORRES

ANGELS PITCHER
JOHN VERHOEVEN

NORM SHERRY MANAGER
ANGELS

1978

The best finish in the club's history occurred in 1978 when the Angels, leading the division as late as Aug. 26, settled for a second-place tie with Texas, five games behind the winning Royals. Dave Garcia's tenure as manager ended late in May when Jim Fregosi, a former Angel, took the reins. Don Baylor had a fine season with 34 homers and 99 RBIs. Back problems restricted Bobby Grich to a .251 average. Rookie Carney Lansford played third and batted .294. First baseman Ron Jackson batted .297 and despite a wrist injury in August knocked in 57 runs. Joe Rudi, also injury-plagued, hit 17 homers and had 79 RBIs. The death of Lyman Bostock, who hit .296, in a September shooting incident cast a pall over the Angels' season. Frank Tanana's 18-12 was tops for the pitchers. Nolan Ryan was 10-13 and Ken Brett 13-8. Chris Knapp won 14 games and relief ace Dave LaRoche had 10 wins and 25 saves.

MIKE BARLOW

DON BAYLOR

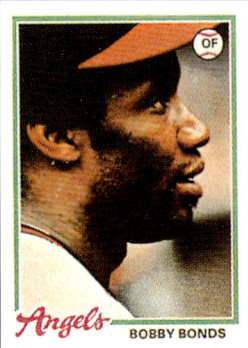
BOBBY BONDS

THAD BOSLEY

LYMAN BOSTOCK

KEN BRETT

DAVE CHALK

ANDY ETCHEBARREN

GIL FLORES

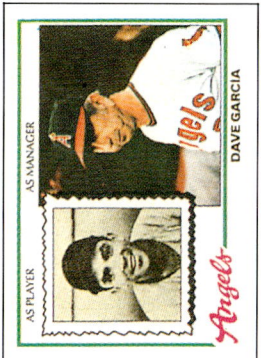

DAVE GARCIA

BOB GRICH

MARIO GUERRERO

IKE HAMPTON

PAUL HARTZELL

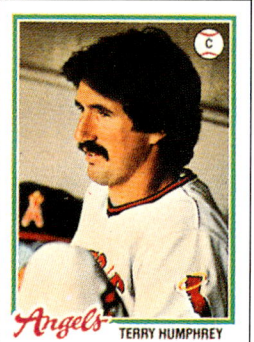

TERRY HUMPHREY

RON JACKSON

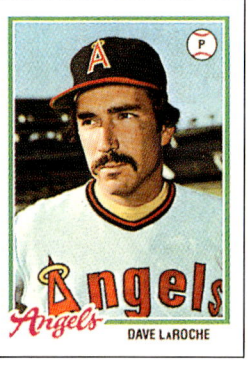

DAVE LaROCHE

DYAR MILLER

BALOR MOORE

RANCE MULLINIKS

GARY NOLAN

JERRY REMY

GARY ROSS

JOE RUDI

★ ★ ★ ★ ★ ★ ★ ★ ★ ★ MOST GAMES,
10-OR-MORE STRIKEOUTS, LIFETIME

'77 RECORD ★ ★ ★ ★ ★ ★ ★ ★ ★
BREAKER NOLAN RYAN

NOLAN RYAN

TONY SOLAITA

FRANK TANANA

1979

Finally, in their 19th season, the Angels rewarded owner Gene Autry with a divisional title in 1979. He had little time to savor it, however, as the Orioles eliminated the Angels in four playoff games. Don Baylor, the league's MVP, hit .296 with 36 home runs and 139 RBIs. Bobby Grich, recovered from his back ailment, stroked 30 homers and had 101 RBIs. Catcher Brian Downing batted .336 and Rod Carew, signed as a free agent, hit .318 despite a lingering thumb problem. Carney Lansford batted .287 and had 19 homers while centerfielder Rick Miller, despite a wrist injury, batted .293.

Manager Jim Fregosi's pitching wasn't of championship caliber. Nolan Ryan, in his farewell Angels season, won 16 and lost 14. Dave Frost went 16-10. Don Aase won nine and lost 10 and Frank Tanana's numbers fell to 7-5. Dave LaRoche was 7-11 as a reliever, but Mark Clear, 11-5, picked up the bullpen slack.

DON AASE P
ANGELS

DON BAYLOR DH-OF
ANGELS

KEN BRETT P
ANGELS

DAVE CHALK 3B
ANGELS

BRIAN DOWNING C
ANGELS

RON FAIRLY DH-1B
ANGELS

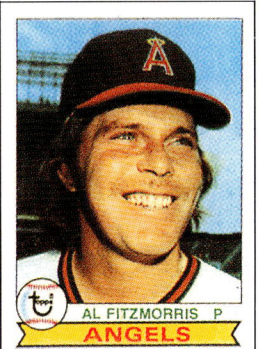

AL FITZMORRIS P
ANGELS

DANNY GOODWIN DH
ANGELS

BOB GRICH 2B
ANGELS

TOM GRIFFIN P
ANGELS

PAUL HARTZELL P
ANGELS

TERRY HUMPHREY C
ANGELS

RON JACKSON 3B-1B
ANGELS

CHRIS KNAPP P
ANGELS

KEN LANDREAUX OF
ANGELS

CARNEY LANSFORD SS-3B
ANGELS

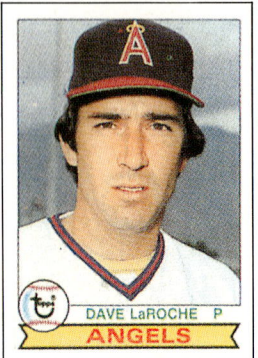

DAVE LaROCHE P
ANGELS

DYAR MILLER P
ANGELS

RICK MILLER OF
ANGELS

MERV RETTENMUND OF
ANGELS

JOE RUDI OF
ANGELS

NOLAN RYAN P
ANGELS

TONY SOLAITA 1B
ANGELS

FRANK TANANA P
ANGELS

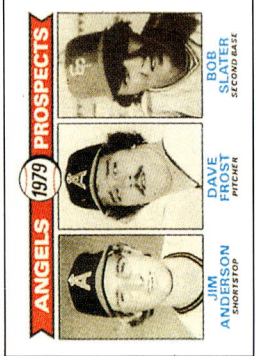

ANGELS PROSPECTS 1979
BOB SLATER SECOND BASE
DAVE FROST PITCHER
JIM ANDERSON SHORTSTOP

ANGELS
JIM FREGOSI MANAGER

1980

Inability to stand prosperity cost the Angels dearly in 1980 as they tumbled from divisional winners to sixth place, 20 games below .500 and 31 lengths behind the winning Royals. Injuries to offensive performers plus a breakdown in pitching doomed the Halos. Don Baylor broke his wrist, Brian Downing an ankle; Dan Ford, hobbled by a knee injury, played only 65 games. Rod Carew batted .331 while Carney Lansford had 15 homers and knocked in 80 runs. The pitching staff wasn't without its ailments, either. Bruce Kison won only three games and Dave Frost four and each suffered physical problems. Frank Tanana ended at 11-12. Mark Clear was 11-11 and Chris Knapp 2-11.

   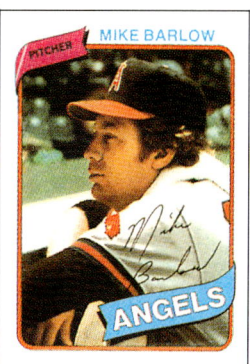

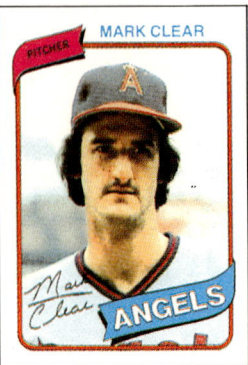
PITCHER MARK CLEAR
ANGELS

CATCHER TOM DONOHUE
ANGELS

CATCHER BRIAN DOWNING
ANGELS

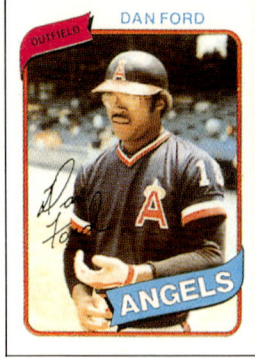
OUTFIELD DAN FORD
ANGELS

PITCHER DAVE FROST
ANGELS

2nd BASE BOB GRICH
ANGELS

OUTFIELD LARRY HARLOW
ANGELS

PITCHER CHRIS KNAPP
ANGELS

3rd BASE CARNEY LANSFORD
ANGELS

PITCHER DAVE LaROCHE
ANGELS

OUTFIELD RICK MILLER
ANGELS

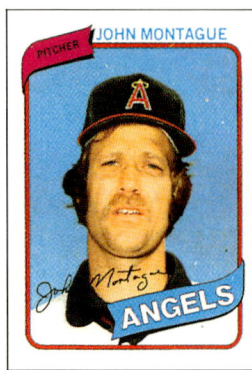
PITCHER JOHN MONTAGUE
ANGELS

OUTFIELD MERV RETTENMUND
ANGELS

OUTFIELD JOE RUDI
ANGELS

PITCHER NOLAN RYAN
★ A.L. ALL-STAR ★
ANGELS

PITCHER FRANK TANANA
ANGELS

1981

It wasn't the mid-season players' strike that hobbled the Angels in 1981 but rather, many observers believe, some of the trades and player acquisitions. The club finished fifth in the overall standings and Jim Fregosi, who got axed as manager in May, had little to do with that. Neither did his successor, Gene Mauch.

Pitchers Bill Travers, Geoff Zahn, John D'Acquisto and Jesse Jefferson were free agents signed for approximately $4 million and none panned out. Travers' arm problem limited him to 9.2 innings, Zahn won 10 and lost 11. D'Acquisto pitched mostly in the minors and Jefferson was an uninspiring 2-4. Ken Forsch won 11 while Mike Witt and Steve Renko each won eight. A January deal brought Fred Lynn from Boston but injuries lowered his average to .219. Rod Carew did hit .305, a point above Bobby Grich. Rick Burleson, obtained from Boston, hit .293.

SHORTSTOP ANGELS
RICK BURLESON

SHORTSTOP ANGELS
BERT CAMPANERIS

A.L. ALL-STAR
1st BASE ANGELS
ROD CAREW

OUTFIELD ANGELS
BOB CLARK

PITCHER ANGELS
MARK CLEAR

CATCHER ANGELS
TOM DONOHUE

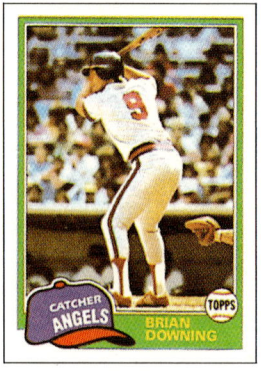

CATCHER ANGELS
BRIAN DOWNING

OUTFIELD ANGELS
DAN FORD

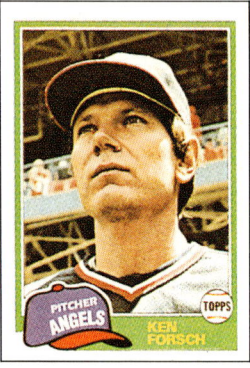

PITCHER ANGELS
KEN FORSCH

PITCHER ANGELS
DAVE FROST

2nd BASE ANGELS
BOB GRICH

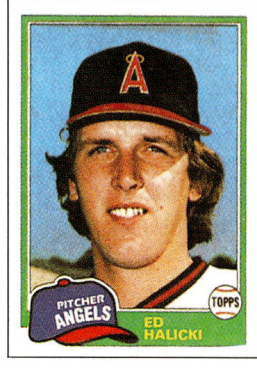

PITCHER ANGELS
ED HALICKI

OUTFIELD ANGELS
LARRY HARLOW

PITCHER ANGELS
ANDY HASSLER

3rd BASE ANGELS
BUTCH HOBSON

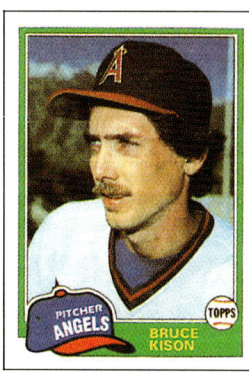

PITCHER ANGELS
BRUCE KISON

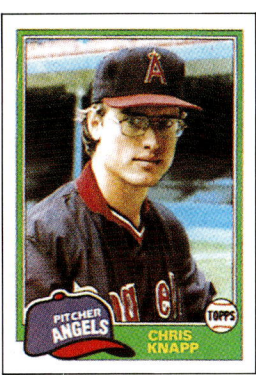

PITCHER
ANGELS
CHRIS
KNAPP

3rd BASE
ANGELS
CARNEY
LANSFORD

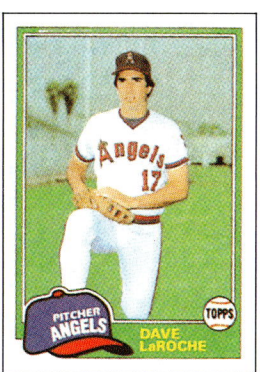

PITCHER
ANGELS
DAVE
LaROCHE

PITCHER
ANGELS
DAVE
LEMANCZYK

OUTFIELD
ANGELS
FRED
LYNN

PITCHER
ANGELS
FRED
MARTINEZ

OUTFIELD
ANGELS
RICK
MILLER

PITCHER
ANGELS
JOHN
MONTAGUE

CATCHER
ANGELS
ED
OTT

SHORTSTOP
ANGELS
FREDDIE
PATEK

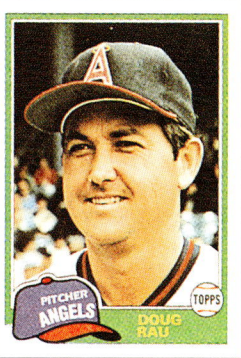

PITCHER
ANGELS
DOUG
RAU

PITCHER
ANGELS
STEVE
RENKO

OUTFIELD
ANGELS
JOE
RUDI

CATCHER
ANGELS
DAVE
SKAGGS

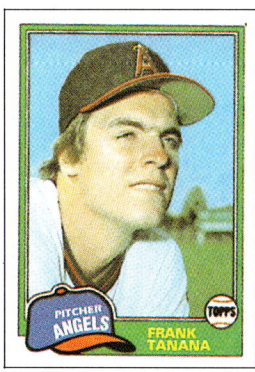

PITCHER
ANGELS
FRANK
TANANA

1st BASE
ANGELS
JASON
THOMPSON

≡1982≡

The Angels' second Western Division title in four season became a reality in 1982 but the euphoria didn't linger as the Halos were eliminated by Milwaukee in the pennant playoff. Signing Reggie Jackson to a free agent contract became a plus when he hit 39 homers to tie for the A.L. lead and also knocked in 101 runs. Bob Boone, acquired from Philadelphia, gave the Angels the defense they sought behind the plate. Rod Carew hit .319 and the newly obtained Doug DeCinces hit .301 plus 30 homers. Infielder Tim Foli, obtained from Pittsburgh, provided the needed infield defense while Brian Downing hit .281 and 28 homers. Fred Lynn, rebounding from his poor 1981 season, hit .299 with 21 home runs. Geoff Zahn won 18 to lead the pitching corps. Ken Forsch was 13-11 and Steve Renko 11-6. Tommy John, acquired from the Yankees late in the season, won four games plus another in the playoffs.

ANGELS
PITCHER · DON AASE

ANGELS
DH-OF · DON BAYLOR

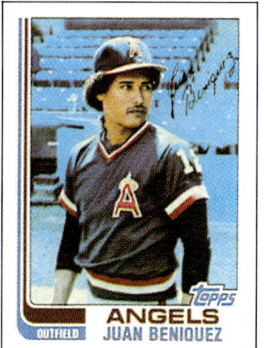

ANGELS
OUTFIELD · JUAN BENIQUEZ

ANGELS
CATCHER · BOB BOONE

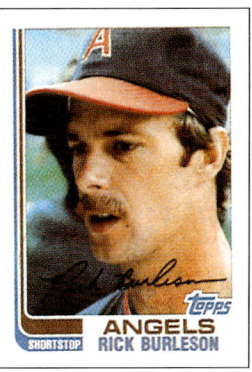

ANGELS
SHORTSTOP · RICK BURLESON

ANGELS
SHORTSTOP · BERT CAMPANERIS

ANGELS
1st BASE · ROD CAREW

ROD CAREW
in action

A.L. ALL STAR
1st BASE · ROD CAREW

ANGELS
OUTFIELD · BOB CLARK

ANGELS
PITCHER · DOUG CORBETT

ANGELS
PITCHER · JOHN D'ACQUISTO

ANGELS
3rd BASE · DOUG DeCINCES

ANGELS
CATCHER · BRIAN DOWNING

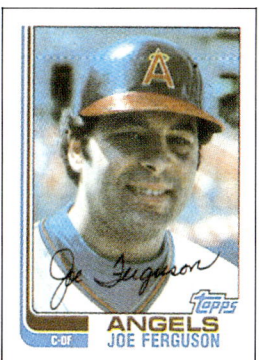

ANGELS
C-OF · JOE FERGUSON

ANGELS
SHORTSTOP · TIM FOLI

ANGELS
OUTFIELD DAN FORD

ANGELS
PITCHER KEN FORSCH

ANGELS
PITCHER DAVE FROST

ANGELS
2nd BASE BOB GRICH

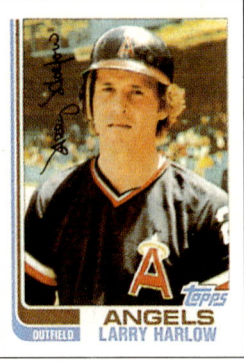

ANGELS
OUTFIELD LARRY HARLOW

ANGELS
1st BASE JOHN HARRIS

ANGELS
PITCHER ANDY HASSLER

ANGELS
3rd BASE BUTCH HOBSON

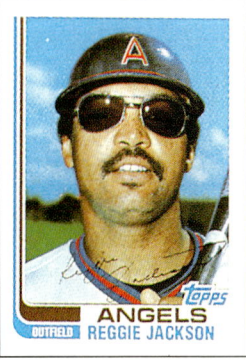

ANGELS
OUTFIELD REGGIE JACKSON

ANGELS
1st BASE RON JACKSON

ANGELS
PITCHER JESSE JEFFERSON

ANGELS
3B-SS MICK KELLEHER

ANGELS
PITCHER BRUCE KISON

ANGELS
OUTFIELD FRED LYNN

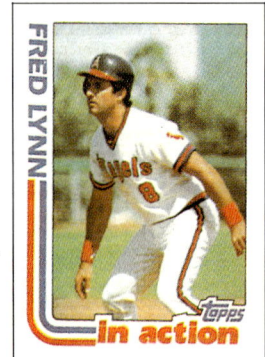

FRED LYNN
in action

ANGELS
PITCHER FRED MARTINEZ

ANGELS
CATCHER
ED OTT

ANGELS
SHORTSTOP
FREDDIE PATEK

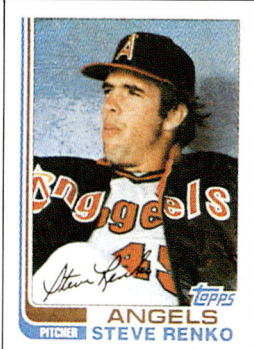

ANGELS
PITCHER
STEVE RENKO

ANGELS
PITCHER
BILL TRAVERS

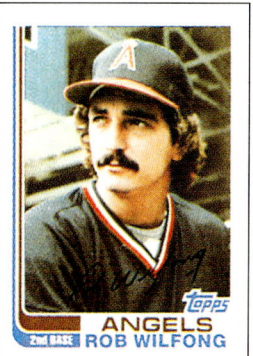

ANGELS
2nd BASE
ROB WILFONG

ANGELS
PITCHER
MIKE WITT

ANGELS
PITCHER
GEOFF ZAHN

CALIFORNIA
ANGELS
'81 BATTING & PITCHING LDRS.
KEN FORSCH · 2.94 ERA
ROD CAREW · .305 BA

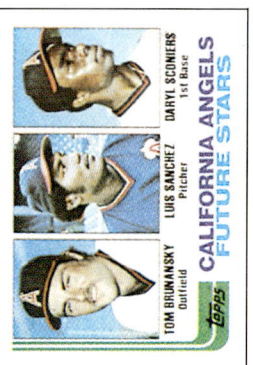

CALIFORNIA ANGELS
FUTURE STARS
DARYL SCONIERS 1st Base
LUIS SANCHEZ Pitcher
TOM BRUNANSKY Outfield

1983

John McNamara managed the Angels in 1983 and to his dismay watched the ballclub lose 92 games and topple into a fifth-place tie with Minnesota. Injuries again hurt the Halos. Bobby Grich, was hitting .292 with 16 homers when a broken hand ended his season in August. Reggie Jackson, nursing a rib problem, batted only .194 with 14 home runs. Rod Carew, off to a blazing start, finished with a .339 average. Rick Burleson hit .286 and Fred Lynn .272. Ken Forsch, Tommy John and Bruce Kison each won 11 games. Luis Sanchez was 10-8 while Geoff Zahn went 9-11 and Mike Witt 7-14.

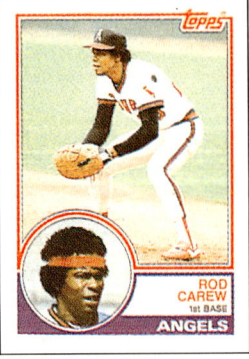

BOB
CLARK
OUTFIELD
ANGELS

DOUG
CORBETT
PITCHER
ANGELS

JOHN
CURTIS
PITCHER
ANGELS

DOUG
DeCINCES
3rd BASE
ANGELS

BRIAN
DOWNING
OUTFIELD
ANGELS

JOE
FERGUSON
CATCHER-OUTFIELD
ANGELS

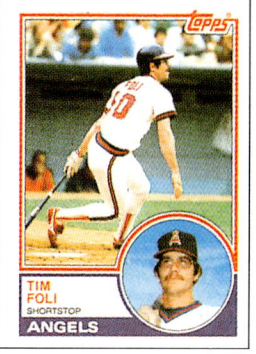

TIM
FOLI
SHORTSTOP
ANGELS

KEN
FORSCH
PITCHER
ANGELS

DAVE
GOLTZ
PITCHER
ANGELS

BOB
GRICH
2ND BASE
ALL STAR
A L

BOB
GRICH
2nd BASE
ANGELS

ANDY
HASSLER
PITCHER
ANGELS

REGGIE
JACKSON
OUTFIELD
ALL STAR
A L

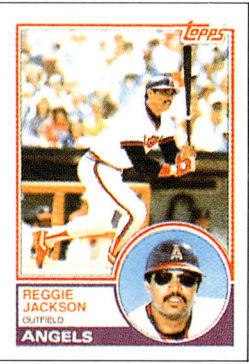

REGGIE
JACKSON
OUTFIELD
ANGELS

SUPER VETERAN
1983
1967
REGGIE JACKSON

RON
JACKSON
1st BASE
ANGELS

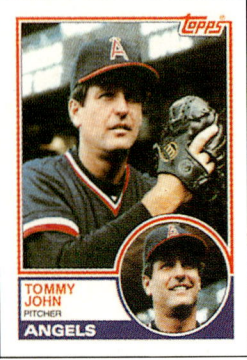
TOMMY
JOHN
PITCHER
ANGELS

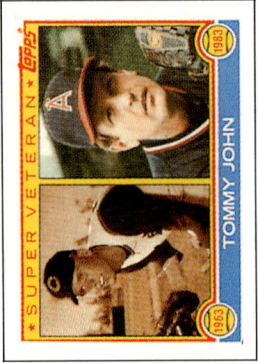
★ SUPER VETERAN ★ TOMMY JOHN

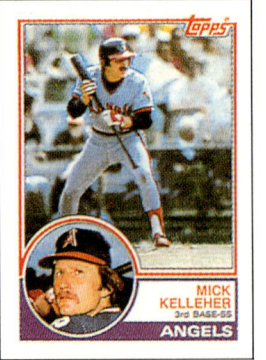
MICK
KELLEHER
3rd BASE-SS
ANGELS

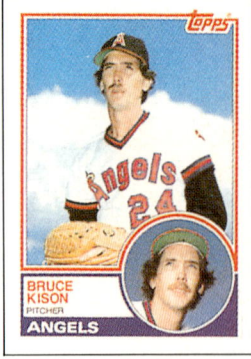
BRUCE
KISON
PITCHER
ANGELS

FRED
LYNN
OUTFIELD
ALL STAR

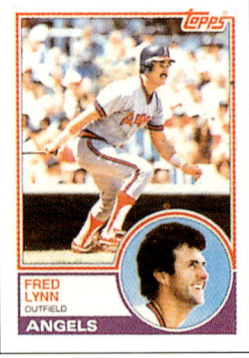
FRED
LYNN
OUTFIELD
ANGELS

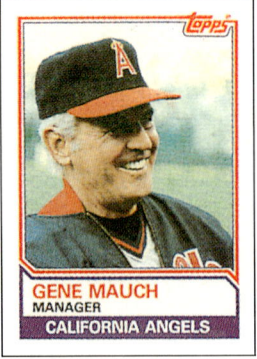
GENE MAUCH
MANAGER
CALIFORNIA ANGELS

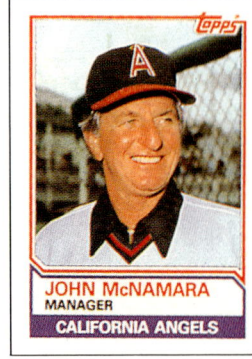
JOHN McNAMARA
MANAGER
CALIFORNIA ANGELS

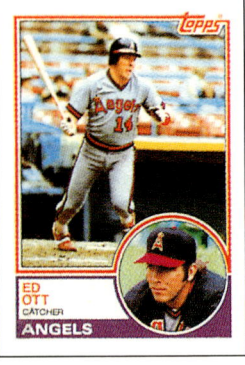
ED OTT
CATCHER
ANGELS

STEVE
RENKO
PITCHER
ANGELS

LUIS
SANCHEZ
PITCHER
ANGELS

DARYL
SCONIERS
1st BASE
ANGELS

LUIS
TIANT
PITCHER
ANGELS

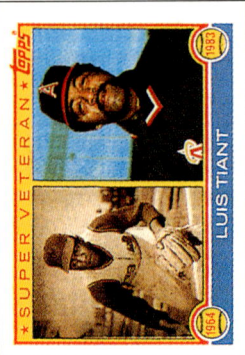
★ SUPER VETERAN ★ LUIS TIANT

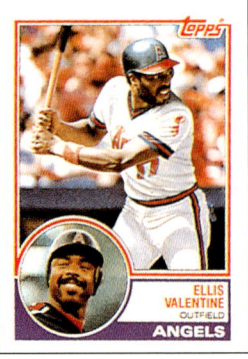
ELLIS
VALENTINE
OUTFIELD
ANGELS

ROB
WILFONG
2nd BASE
ANGELS

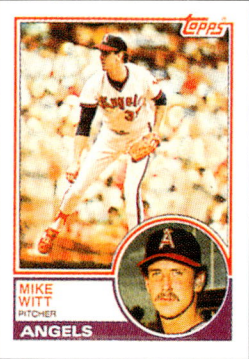

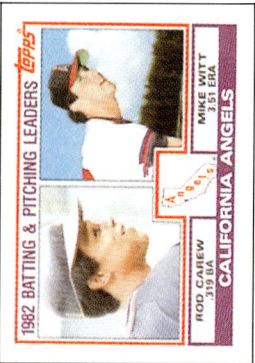

1984

The Angels tied with the Twins for second place, three games behind Kansas City in 1984, but that didn't prevent John McNamara from resigning as skipper following the season. The club contended until July but then virtually everything misfired in the final months.

Reggie Jackson rebounded to hit 25 homers and Rod Carew batted .295, the first year he didn't reach .300 since 1968. Bob Boone hit only .202 and rookie shortstop Rick Schofield a meager .193. Doug DeCinces hit 20 homers, Brian Downing hit 19 and Fred Lynn 22. Mike Witt, who climaxed the season with a perfect-game win over Texas, was the Angels' ace with 15 wins. Geoff Zahn won 13 and young Mike Romanick was 12-12. Tommy John won seven and Luis Sanchez nine. Don Aase and Doug Corbett, a tandem out of the 'pen, combined for nine victories and a dozen saves.

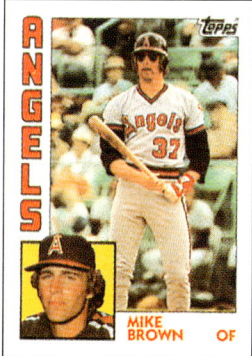

RICK BURLESON SS

ROD CAREW 1B

BOB CLARK OF

JOHN CURTIS P

DOUG DeCINCES 3B

BRIAN DOWNING OF

TIM FOLI SS

KEN FORSCH P

BOB GRICH 2B

ANDY HASSLER P

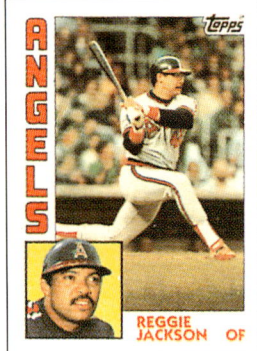

REGGIE JACKSON OF

RON JACKSON 3B-1B

TOMMY JOHN P

BRUCE KISON P

FRANK LaCORTE P

STEVE LUBRATICH 3B-SS-2B

FRED LYNN OF

BYRON McLAUGHLIN P

MANAGER
JOHN McNAMARA

MIKE O'BERRY C

GARY PETTIS OF

ROB PICCIOLO SS-2B

RON ROMANICK P

LUIS SANCHEZ P

DICK SCHOFIELD SS

DARYL SCONIERS 1B

JIM SLATON P

CRAIG SWAN P

ELLIS VALENTINE OF

ROB WILFONG 2B

MIKE WITT P

GEOFF ZAHN P

1985

Gene Mauch returned as manager in 1985 and though his team was universally relegated to the second division, he astounded the baseball world by finishing second, only one game behind Kansas City. The Angels batted a league-high .251 and hit 153 home runs. The pitching staff's ERA of 3.91 was only fifth best in the league but Mauch still managed to contend. Juan Beniquez, a utility player, hit .304 and among the regulars Rod Carew's .280 was the best. Reggie Jackson hit 27 homers and shared the club's RBI lead with Brian Downing at 85.

Mike Witt, 15-9, was again the pitching ace. Mike Romanick won 14 and young Kirk McCaskill 12. Stew Cliburn won nine and Donnie Moore dominated the relievers with eight wins and 31 saves.

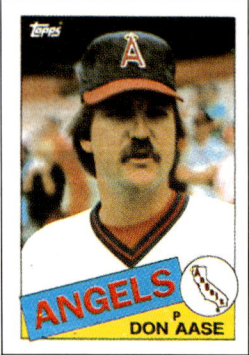

ANGELS
1B ROD CAREW

ANGELS
P DOUG CORBETT

ANGELS
3B DOUG DeCINCES

ANGELS
OF BRIAN DOWNING

ANGELS
P KEN FORSCH

ANGELS
2B BOB GRICH

ANGELS
DH REGGIE JACKSON

ANGELS
P TOMMY JOHN

ANGELS
P CURT KAUFMAN

ANGELS
P BRUCE KISON

ANGELS
P FRANK LaCORTE

ANGELS
OF FRED LYNN

ANGELS
MANAGER JOHN McNAMARA

ANGELS
C-1B JERRY NARRON

ANGELS
OF GARY PETTIS

ANGELS
SS-2B ROB PICCIOLO

ANGELS
P
RON ROMANICK

ANGELS
P
LUIS SANCHEZ

ANGELS
SS
DICK SCHOFIELD

ANGELS
1B
DARYL SCONIERS

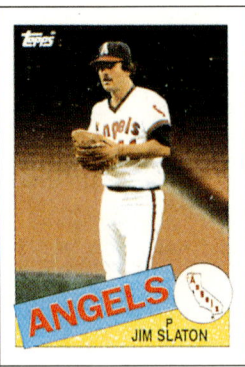
ANGELS
P
JIM SLATON

ANGELS
2B
ROB WILFONG

ANGELS
MIKE WITT

ANGELS
P
GEOFF ZAHN

1986

The Angels won their third Western Division title in eight seasons but again were denied the pennant when they dropped a seven-game playoff to Boston in 1986. California had four pitchers win in double figures with Mike Witt (18-10) the top hurler. Kirk McCaskill went 17-10 and the veteran Don Sutton 15-11. John Candelaria, recovering from a lingering arm ailment, won 10 of 12 decisions and Donnie Moore, the bullpen star, registered 21 saves.

Rookie first baseman Wally Joyner hit .290 and was the Angels' top batsman. The youngster cracked 22 home runs and led the club in RBIs with 100. Doug DeCinces hit 26 homers and had 96 RBIs. Brian Downing had 20 homers and 95 RBIs while Reggie Jackson, in what many believed might be his final season, hit 18 homers and drove in 58 runs.

JUAN BENIQUEZ

BOB BOONE

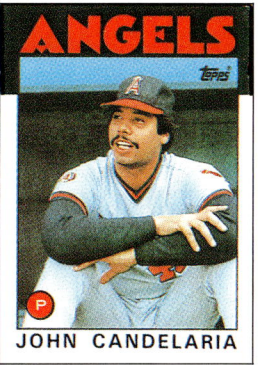

JOHN CANDELARIA

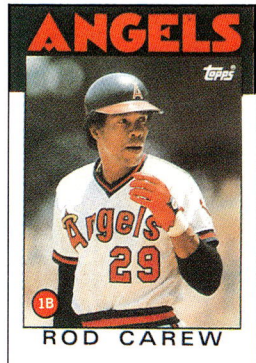

ROD CAREW

PAT CLEMENTS

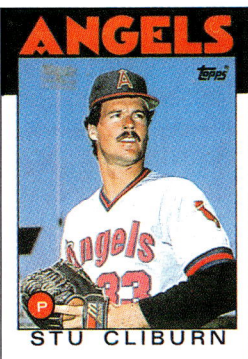

STU CLIBURN

DOUG CORBETT

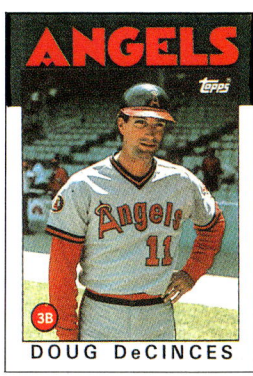

DOUG DeCINCES

BRIAN DOWNING

CRAIG GERBER

BOB GRICH

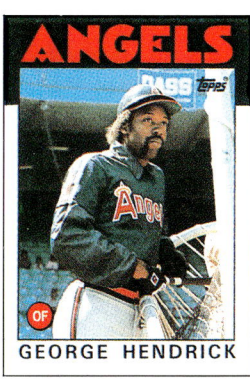

GEORGE HENDRICK

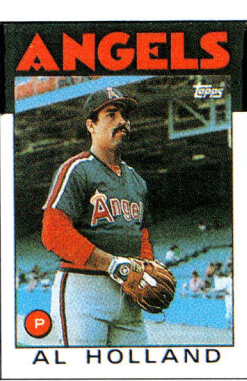

AL HOLLAND

JACK HOWELL

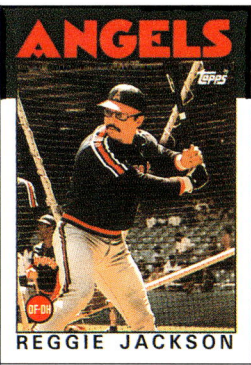

REGGIE JACKSON

RUPPERT JONES

RUPPERT JONES

URBANO LUGO

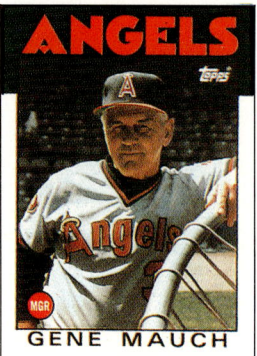

GENE MAUCH

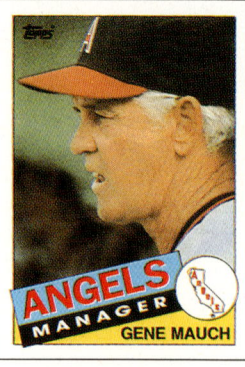

ANGELS MANAGER
GENE MAUCH

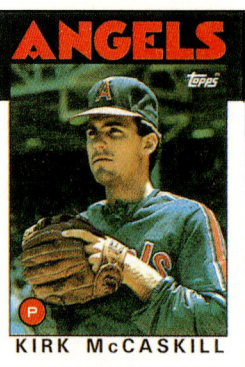

KIRK McCASKILL

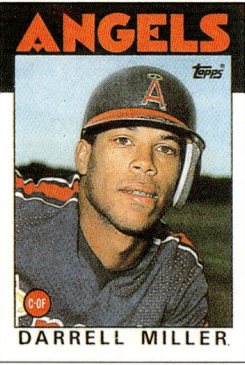

DARRELL MILLER

ANGELS
DONNIE MOORE

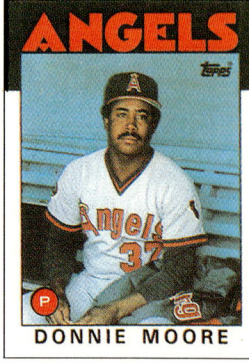

DONNIE MOORE

JERRY NARRON

GARY PETTIS

RON ROMANICK

LUIS SANCHEZ

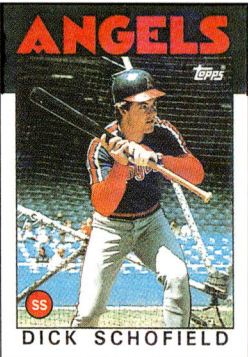

DICK SCHOFIELD

DARYL SCONIERS

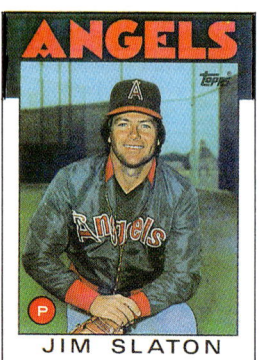

JIM SLATON

DON SUTTON

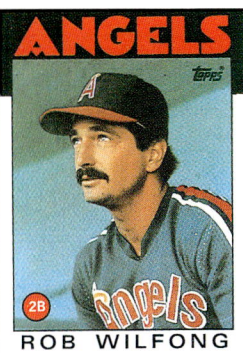
ROB WILFONG

GEOFF ZAHN

ANGELS LEADERS

≡1987≡

It was a season of milestones for many of the California Angels but the team as a whole was unable to overcome injuries to key pitchers to defend its division crown.

Catcher Bob Boone became baseball's all-time leader in games caught during the season and pitcher Don Sutton finished 11-11 to raise his career victory total to 321.

Brian Downing also had another productive year, finishing with 106 walks (tied for the league lead), scoring 110 runs (tied for third in the league). Downing hit .272 with 29 homers (second on the club) and 77 RBI. He was also hit 17 times by pitches, the league's second highest total.

First baseman Wally Joyner defied the "sophomore jinx" by having another super season. Joyner hit .285 with a club-high 34 homers and 117 RBI (fourth best in the league).

A strong addition late in the season was second baseman Johnny Ray, acquired from the Pittsburgh Pirates. Ray, one of the game's best defensive players, hit .346 after joining the Angels in late August.

Devon White also developed into star status in center field with a.263 average, 24 homers and 87 RBI to go with his superb defensive ability.

White's development made Gary Pettis available for a trade and, following the season, Pettis was dealt to Detroit for veteran pitcher Dan Petry.

One of the interesting developments during the season was manager Gene Mauch's offensive strategy. Although much of baseball was preoccupied with the home runs hit during the season, Mauch milked as much production out of his offensive opportunities as possible with sacrifice bunts. Three Angels ranked in the top five in the league in that department — Mark McLemore (15), Boone (14) and White (14).

Kirk McCaskill, one of the keys to the Angels' pitching, underwent elbow surgery and appeared in only 14 games.

Among the healthy pitchers, Mike Witt was 16-14 with a 4.01 ERA and rookie Willie Fraser made a positive impression with a 10-10 record and a 3.92 ERA when McCaskill went down.

Another big surprise was the bull pen performance by DeWayne Buice, a 10-year veteran of the minor leagues, who led the club with 17 saves. Greg Minton had 10 saves.

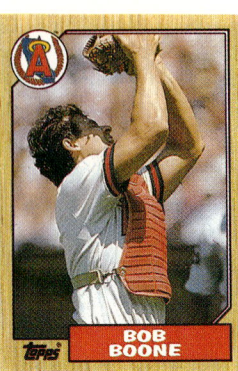

BOB BOONE

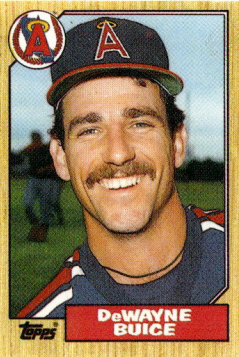

DeWAYNE BUICE

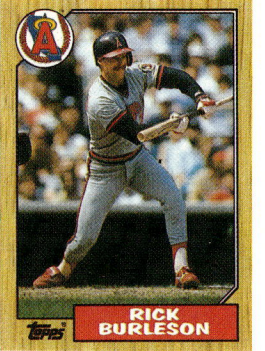

RICK BURLESON

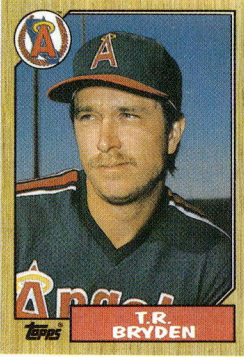

T.R. BRYDEN

JOHN CANDELARIA

DOUG CORBETT

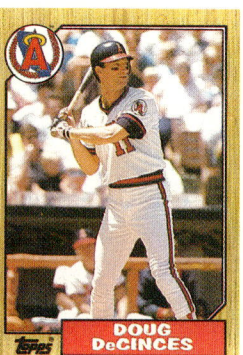

DOUG DeCINCES

BRIAN DOWNING

CHUCK FINLEY

TERRY FORSTER

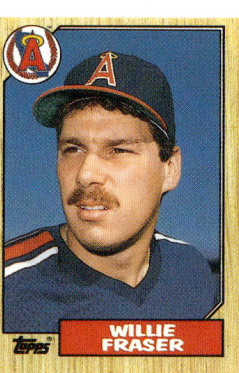

WILLIE FRASER

BOB GRICH

GEORGE HENDRICK

JACK HOWELL

REGGIE JACKSON

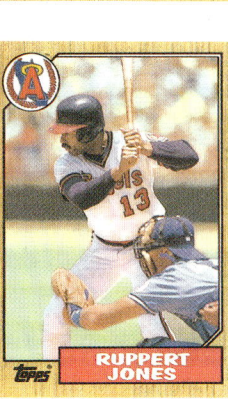

RUPPERT JONES

WALLY JOYNER

JACK LAZORKO

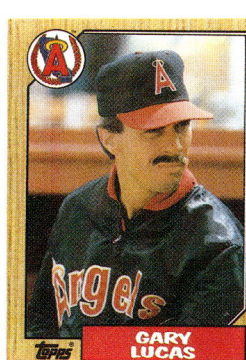
GARY LUCAS

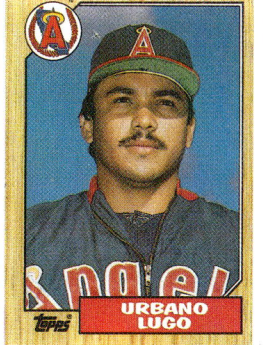
URBANO LUGO

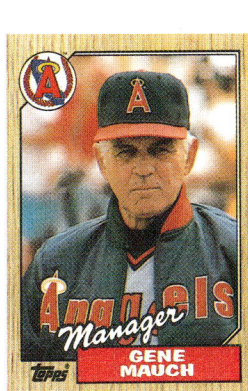
GENE MAUCH

KIRK McCASKILL

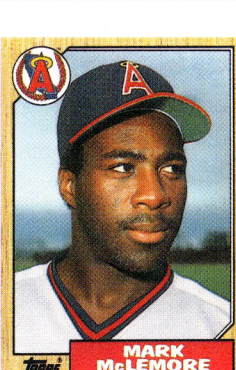
MARK McLEMORE

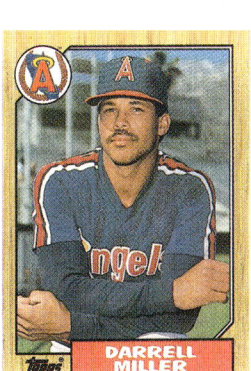
DARRELL MILLER

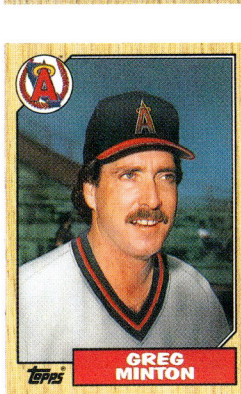
GREG MINTON

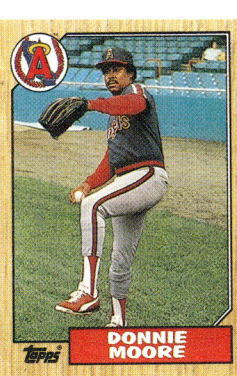
DONNIE MOORE

JERRY NARRON

GARY PETTIS

RON ROMANICK

VERN RUHLE

DICK SCHOFIELD

DON SUTTON

DEVON WHITE

ROB WILFONG

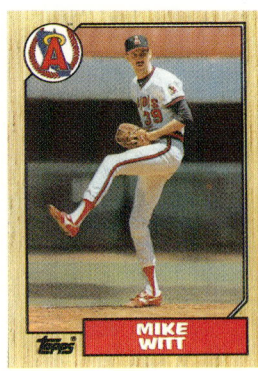

MIKE WITT

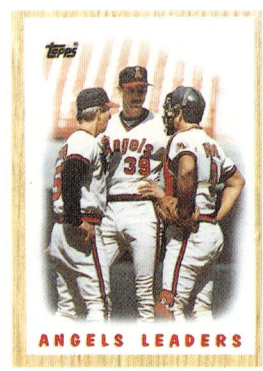

ANGELS LEADERS

1988

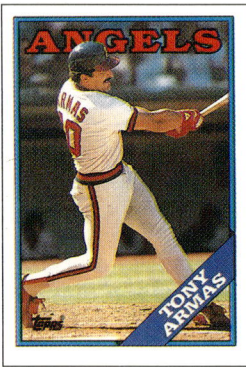

TONY ARMAS

BOB BOONE

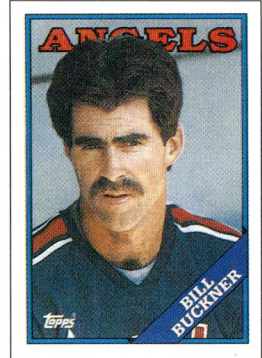

BILL BUCKNER

DeWAYNE BUICE

DOUG DeCINCES

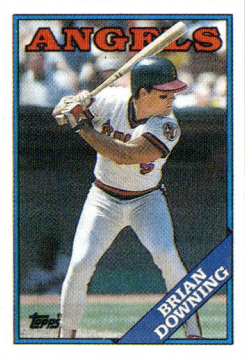

BRIAN DOWNING

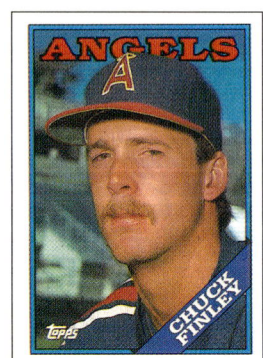

CHUCK FINLEY

WILLIE FRASER

GEORGE HENDRICK

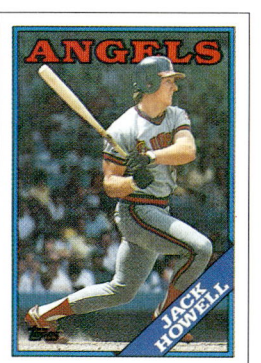
JACK HOWELL

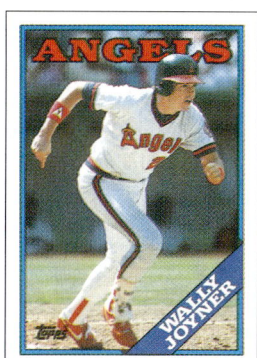
WALLY JOYNER

JACK LAZORKO

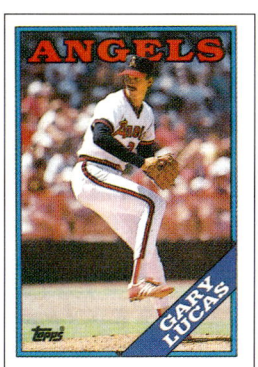
GARY LUCAS

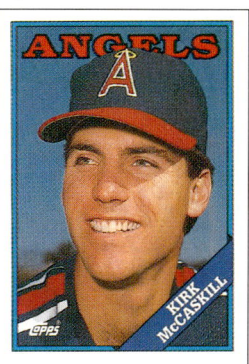
KIRK McCASKILL

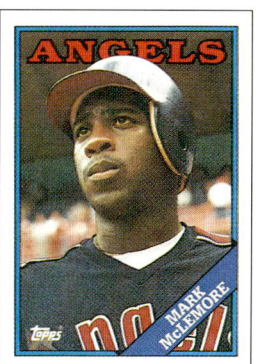
MARK McLEMORE

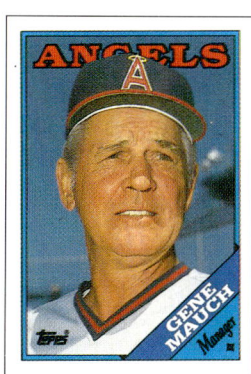
GENE MAUCH

DARRELL MILLER

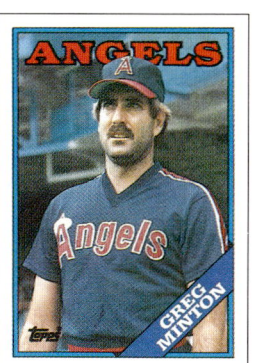
GREG MINTON

DONNIE MOORE

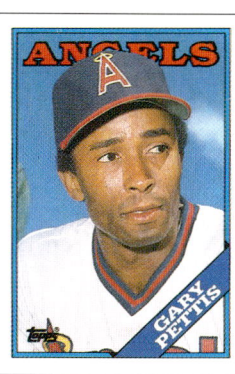
GARY PETTIS

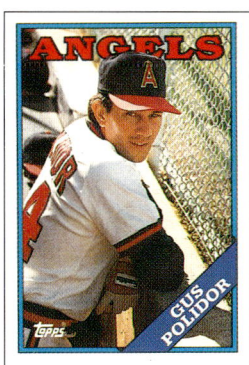
GUS POLIDOR

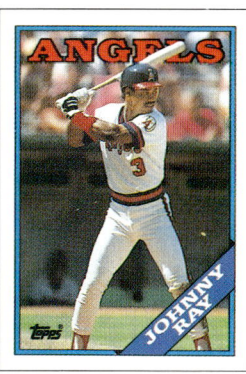
JOHNNY RAY

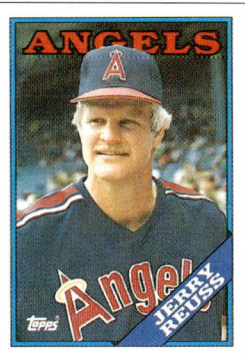
JERRY REUSS

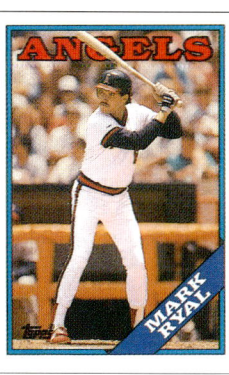
MARK RYAL

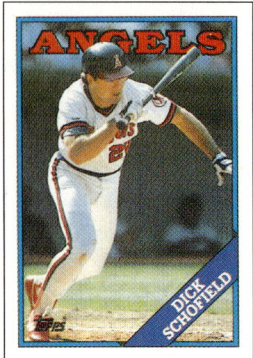

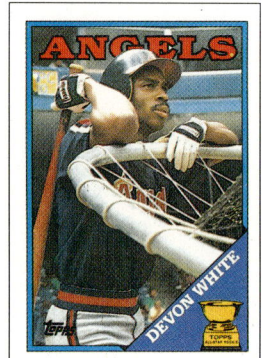
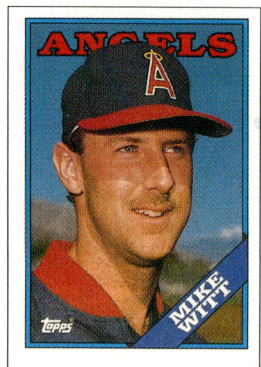

ALEX JOHNSON

Alex Johnson is the only player to win a batting title and to reach the 200-hit plateau for the Angels. The muscular outfielder hit a career high .329 to lead the league in 1970.

In one of the narrowest races in American League history, Johnson's two-for-three afternoon in the season's finale, which gave him his 202 safeties, enabled Alex to nip Boston's Carl Yastrzemski by .003 points for the coveted batting crown.

Johnson was particularly effective in September, hitting .381. A 12-game hitting streak, during which he batted .468, enabled him to terminate his season on the highest note.

Alex's season-long consistency is evidenced by the fact he batted .327 at home and .331 on the road. He hit .329 prior to the All-Star break and .330 following it. As for lefty-righty pitching, Johnson, though a righthanded batter, hit .335 against righthanders and .315 vs southpaws.

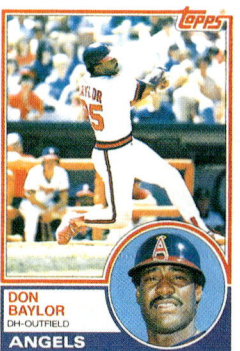

DON BAYLOR

During his six-season stay with the Angels, Don Baylor left an indelible mark with what he accomplished on and off the field. An outfielder, first baseman, sometime designated hitter and always a class person, Baylor was the catalyst of the Angels' Western Division title in 1979.

The American League's Most Valuable Player that year, Don earned his accolade with some stunning performances. He led the majors in runs scored (120) and RBIs (139). In May, when he hit .354 and July (.349) he was named the A.L. Player of the Month, the only player to earn that honor more than once.

A .296 hitter for the 1979 season, Baylor, while assaying the demanding and exacting role of designated hitter, stroked .349 and hit 22 of his 36 home runs while accounting for 66 RBIs.

The Angels' player representative, Baylor was instrumental in launching the "65 Roses Sports Club" — a branch of Cystic Fibrosis. The clubs are now recognized on a national basis.

NOLAN RYAN

Nolan Ryan, the majors' all-time strikeout leader, pitched eight years for the Angels (1972-1979) and in each made a unique contribution that brought fame to himself and his club.

In seven of his seasons with the Angels, Nolan led the American League in strikeouts, four times exceeding 300, including 1973 when he fanned an all-time record 383 batters.

Ryan pitched four no-hitters for the Angels and during his tenure held or tied 26 club records, including league standards for 10 or more K's in a game (114) and most times 15 or more strikeouts in an outing (19).

Twice a 20-game winner, Ryan pitched six one-hitters, 13 two-hitters and 20 three-hitters for the Angels. In 1974 he was twice officially clocked at throwing his famed fastball at over 100 miles per hour.

BOBBY GRICH

When the California Angels launched their Hall of Fame it seemed more than fitting that Bobby Grich should be the inaugural entrant. He wasn't the greatest player in the club's history but Grich's 10 seasons in Anaheim were marked by persistence, production and performance.

Signed as a free agent after he exited Baltimore following the 1976 season, Grich, despite recurring back problems, gave the Angels a major league effort. Primarily a second baseman, Bobby established or equalled a host of fielding marks while performing in a club record 1,098 games at that position.

A career .266 batter, Grich, though never considered one of the league's boppers, hit 154 four baggers as an Angel and in the strike-shortened 1981 season shared the A.L. home run title when he hit 22.

DEAN CHANCE

The media now calls it a career year and when Dean Chance's 1964 season for the Angels is spotlighted, more than a few would agree it epitomized the phrase.

An original Angel — he was drafted from Baltimore in 1960 — Chance was 20-9 in 1964 and his 1.65 ERA has been bettered only once in the 23 years that have elapsed.

In addition Chance authored 11 shutouts, including a record-tying five by 1-0 scores. Named No. 1 on 17 of the 20 Cy Young ballots in 1964, Dean led A.L. pitchers with 278 innings worked and 15 complete games. Along with five two-hitters, a three-hitter, a quartet of four-hitters and one five-hitter, the tall righthander was unbeaten from July 11 to August 18, winning nine games.

A 5-5 pitcher at the All-Star break, Chance, 11-3 with a 1.08 ERA at home in 1964, dominated moundsmen over the second half, going 15-4 with a nifty 1.29 ERA over that span.

ROD CAREW

When Rod Carew becomes eligible for the Hall of Fame election in 1991 it's a virtual certainty this Angels' star will make Cooperstown on the initial ballot.

With 3,053 career basehits, a lifetime .328 average and seven American League batting titles, his credentials are solid. A .300 hitter for 15 straight years, Carew batted .314 in his seven California seasons.

A 15-time member of the All Star team — six with the Angels — Rod led American League first baseman no fewer than half a dozen times in the fan balloting. With over 33 million total votes in his career, Carew leads all major leaguers in that balloting.

Rod was the first Angels' player to have his uniform number retired. That was accomplished at a special ceremony, August 12, 1986 at Anaheim, when the retired Carew and his famed No. 29 were honored.

1951: Blue Back of Johnny Mize (50) lists for $25 . . . Red Back of Duke Snider (38) lists for $18 . . . Complete set of 9 Team Cards lists for $900 . . . Complete set of 11 Connie Mack All-Stars lists for $2750 with Babe Ruth and Lou Gehrig listing for $700 each . . . Current All-Stars of Jim Konstanty, Robin Roberts and Eddie Stanky list for $4000 each . . . Complete set lists for $14,250.

1952: Mickey Mantle (311) is unquestionably the most sought-after post-war gum card, reportedly valued at $6,500-plus . . . Ben Chapman (391) is photo of Sam Chapman . . . Complete set lists in excess of $36,000.

1953: Mickey Mantle (82) and Willie Mays (244) list for $1,500 each . . . Set features first TOPPS card of Hall-of-Famer Whitey Ford (207) and only TOPPS card of Hall-of-Famer Satchel Paige (220). Pete Runnels (219) is photo of Don Johnson . . . Complete set lists for $9,500.

1954: Ted Williams is depicted on two cards (1 and 250) . . . Set features rookie cards of Hank Aaron (128), Ernie Banks (94) and Al Kaline (201) . . . Card of Aaron lists for $650 . . . Card of Willie Mays (90) lists for $200 . . . Complete set lists for $5,500.

1955: Set features rookie cards of Sandy Koufax (123), Harmon Killebrew (124) and Roberto Clemente (164) . . . The Clemente and Willie Mays (194) cards list for $425 each . . .Complete set lists for $3,900.

1956: Set features rookie cards of Hall-of-Famers Will Harridge (1), Warren Giles (2), Walter Alston (8) and Luis Aparicio (292) . . . Card of Mickey Mantle (135) lists for $650 . . . Card of Willie Mays (130) lists for $125 . . . Complete set lists for $4,000 . . . The Team Cards are found both dated (1955) and undated and are valued at $15 (dated) and more . . . There are two unnumbered Checklist Cards valued high.

1957: Set features rookie cards of Don Drysdale (18), Frank Robinson (35) and Brooks Robinson (328) . . . A reversal of photo negative made Hank Aaron (20) appear as a left-handed batter . . . Card of Mickey Mantle (95) lists for $600 . . . Cards of Brooks Robinson and Sandy Koufax (302) list for $275 each . . . Complete set lists for $4,800.

1958: Set features first TOPPS cards of Casey Stengel (475) and Stan Musial (476) . . . Mike McCormick (37) is photo of Ray Monzant . . . Milt Bolling (188) is photo of Lou Berberet . . . Bob Smith (226) is photo of Bobby Gene Smith . . . Card of Mickey Mantle (150) lists for $400 . . . Card of Ted Williams (1) lists for $325 . . . Complete set lists for $4,800.

1959: In a notable error, Lou Burdette (440) is shown posing as a left-handed pitcher . . . Set features rookie card of Bob Gibson (514) . . . Ralph Lumenti (316) is photo of Camilo Pascual . . . Card of Gibson lists for $200 . . . Card of Mickey Mantle (10) lists for $300 . . . Complete set lists for $3,000.

1960: A run of 32 consecutively numbered rookie cards (117-148) includes the first card of Carl Yastrzemski (148) . . . J.C. Martin (346) is photo of Gary Peters . . . Gary Peters (407) is photo of J.C. Martin . . . Card of Yastrzemski lists for $150 . . . Card of Mickey Mantle (350) lists for $300 . . . Complete set lists for $2,600.

1961: The Warren Spahn All-Star (589) should have been numbered 587 . . . Set features rookie cards of Billy Williams (141) and Juan Marichal (417) . . . Dutch Dotterer (332) is photo of his brother, Tommy . . . Card of Mickey Mantle (300) lists for $200 . . . Card of Carl Yastrzemski (287) lists for $90 . . . Complete set lists for $3,600.

1962: Set includes special Babe Ruth feature (135-144) . . . some Hal Reniff cards numbered 139 should be 159 . . . Set features rookie card of Lou Brock (387) . . . Gene Freese (205) is shown posing as a left-handed batter . . . Card of Mickey Mantle (200) lists for $325 . . . Card of Carl Yastrzemski (425) lists for $125 . . . Complete set lists for $3,300.

1963: Set features rookie card of Pete Rose (537), which lists for $500-plus . . . Bob Uecker (126) is shown posing as a left-handed batter . . . Don Landrum (113) is photo of Ron Santo . . . Eli Grba (231) is photo of Ryne Duren . . . Card of Mickey Mantle (200) lists for $200 . . . Card of Lou Brock (472) lists for $75 . . . Complete set lists for $2,900.

1964: Set features rookie cards of Richie Allen (243), Tony Conigliaro (287) and Phil Niekro (541) . . . Lou Burdette is again shown posing as a left-handed pitcher . . . Bud Bloomfield (532) is photo of Jay Ward . . . Card of Pete Rose (125) lists for $150 . . . Card of Mickey Mantle (50) lists for $175 . . . Complete set lists for $1,600.

1965: Set features rookie cards of Dave Johnson (473), Steve Carlton (477) and Jim Hunter (526) . . . Lew Krausse (462) is photo of Pete Lovrich . . . Gene Freese (492) is again shown posing as a left-handed batter . . . Cards of Carlton and Pete Rose (207) list for $135 . . . Card of Mickey Mantle (350) lists for $300 . . . Complete set lists for $800.

1966: Set features rookie card of Jim Palmer (126) . . . For the third time (see 1962 and 1965) Gene Freese (319) is shown posing as a left-handed batter . . . Dick Ellsworth (447) is photo of Ken Hubbs (died February 13, 1964) . . . Card of Gaylord Perry (598) lists for $175 . . . Card of Willie McCovey (550) lists for $80 . . . Complete set lists for $2,500.

1967: Set features rookie cards of Rod Carew (569) and Tom Seaver (581) . . . Jim Fregosi (385) is shown posing as a left-handed batter . . . George Korince (72) is photo of James Brown but was later corrected on a second Korince card (526) . . . Card of Carew lists for $150 . . . Card of Maury Wills (570) lists for $65 . . . Complete set lists for $2,500.

1968: Set features rookie cards of Nolan Ryan (177) and Johnny Bench (247) . . . The special feature of The Sporting News All-Stars (361-380) includes eight players in the Hall of Fame . . . Card of Ryan lists for $135 . . . Card of Bench lists for $125 . . . Complete set lists for $1,200.

1969: Set features rookie card of Reggie Jackson (260) . . . There are two poses each for Clay Dalrymple (151) and Donn Clendenon (208) . . . Aurelio Rodriguez (653) is photo of Lenny Garcia (Angels' bat boy) . . . Card of Mickey Mantle (500) lists for $150 . . . Card of Jackson lists for $175 . . . Complete set lists for $1,200.

1970: Set features rookie cards of Vida Blue (21), Thurman Munson (189) and Bill Buckner (286) . . . Also included are two deceased players Miguel Fuentes (88) and Paul Edmondson (414) who died after cards went to press . . . Card of Johnny Bench (660) lists for $75 . . . Card of Pete Rose (580) lists for $75 . . . Complete set lists for $1,000.

1971: Set features rookie card of Steve Garvey (341) . . . the final series (644-752) is found in lesser quantity and includes rookie card (664) of three pitchers named Reynolds (Archie, Bob and Ken) . . . Card of Garvey lists for $65 . . . Card of Pete Rose (100) lists for $45 . . . Complete set lists for $1,000.

1972: There were 16 cards featuring photos of players in their boyhood years . . . Dave Roberts (91) is photo of Danny Coombs . . . Brewers Rookie Card (162) includes photos of Darrell Porter and Jerry Bell, which were reversed . . . Cards of Steve Garvey (686) and Rod Carew (695) list for $60 . . . Card of Pete Rose (559) lists for $50 . . . Complete set lists for $1,000.

1973: A special Home Run Card (1) depicted Babe Ruth, Hank Aaron and Willie Mays . . . Set features rookie card of Mike Schmidt (615) listing for $175 . . . Joe Rudi (360) is photo of Gene Tenace . . . Card of Pete Rose (130) lists for $18 . . . Card of Reggie Jackson (255) lists for $12.50 . . . Complete set lists for $600.

1974: Set features 15 San Diego Padres cards printed as ''Washington, N.L.'' due to report of franchise move, later corrected . . . Also included was a 44-card Traded Series which updated team changes . . . Set features rookie card of Dave Winfield (456) . . . Card of Mike Schmidt (283) lists for $35 . . . Card of Winfield lists for $25 . . . Complete set lists for $325.

1975: Herb Washington (407) is the only card ever published with position ''designated runner,'' featuring only base-running statistics . . . Set features rookie cards of Robin Yount (223), George Brett (228), Jim Rice (616), Gary Carter (620) and Keith Hernandez (623) . . . Don Wilson (455) died after cards went to press (January 5, 1975) . . . Card of Brett lists for $50 . . . Cards of Rice and Carter list for $35 . . . Complete set lists for $475 . . . TOPPS also tested the complete 660-card series in a smaller size (2¼" x 3 1/8") in certain areas of USA in a limited supply . . . Complete set of ''Mini-Cards'' lists for $700.

1976: As in 1974 there was a 44-card Traded Series . . . Set features five Father & Son cards (66-70) and ten All-Time All-Stars (341-350) . . . Card of Pete Rose (240) lists for $15 . . . Cards of Jim Rice (340), Gary Carter (441) and George Brett (19) list for $12 . . . Complete set lists for $225.

1977: Set features rookie cards of Andre Dawson (473) and Dale Murphy (476) . . . Reuschel Brother Combination (634) shows the two (Paul and Rick) misidentified . . . Dave Collins (431) is photo of Bob Jones . . . Card of Murphy lists for $65 . . . Card of Pete Rose (450) lists for $8.50 . . . Complete set lists for $250.

1978: Record Breakers (1-7) feature Lou Brock, Sparky Lyle, Willie McCovey, Brooks Robinson, Pete Rose, Nolan Ryan and Reggie Jackson . . . Set features rookie cards of Jack Morris (703), Lou Whitaker (704), Paul Molitor/Alan Trammell (707), Lance Parrish (708) and Eddie Murray (36) . . . Card of Murray lists for $35 . . . Card of Parrish lists for $35 . . . Complete set lists for $200.

1979: Bump Wills (369) was originally shown with Blue Jays affiliation but later corrected to Rangers . . . Set features rookie cards of Ozzie Smith (116), Pedro Guerrero (719), Lonnie Smith (722) and Terry Kennedy (724) . . . Larry Cox (489) is photo of Dave Rader . . . Card of Dale Murphy (39) lists for $8 . . . Cards of Ozzie Smith and Eddie Murray (640) list for $7.50 . . . Complete set lists for $135.

1980: Highlights (1-6) feature Hall-of-Famers Lou Brock, Carl Yastrzemski, Willie McCovey and Pete Rose . . . Set features rookie cards of Dave Stieb (77), Rickey Henderson (482) and Dan Quisenberry (667) . . . Card of Henderson lists for $28 . . . Card of Dale Murphy (274) lists for $5.50 . . . Complete set lists for $135.

1981: Set features rookie cards of Fernando Valenzuela (302), Kirk Gibson (315), Harold Baines (347) and Tim Raines (479) . . . Jeff Cox (133) is photo of Steve McCatty . . . John Littlefield (489) is photo of Mark Riggins . . . Card of Valenzuela lists for $7.50 . . . Card of Raines lists for $9 . . . Complete set lists for $80.

1982: Pascual Perez (383) printed with no position on front lists for $35, later corrected . . . Set features rookie cards of Cal Ripken (21), Jesse Barfield (203), Steve Sax (681) and Kent Hrbek (766) . . . Dave Rucker (261) is photo of Roger Weaver . . . Steve Bedrosian (502) is photo of Larry Owen . . . Card of Ripken lists for $12.50 . . . Cards of Barfield and Sax list for $5 . . . Complete set lists for $75.

1983: Record Breakers (1-6) feature Tony Armas, Rickey Henderson, Greg Minton, Lance Parrish, Manny Trillo and John Wathan . . . A series of Super Veterans features early and current photos of 34 leading players . . . Set features rookie cards of Tony Gwynn (482) and Wade Boggs (498) . . . Card of Boggs lists for $32 . . . Card of Gwynn lists for $16 . . . Complete set lists for $85.

1984: Highlights (1-6) salute eleven different players . . . A parade of superstars is included in Active Leaders (701-718) . . . Set features rookie card of Don Mattingly (8) listing for $35 . . . Card of Darryl Strawberry (182) lists for $10 . . . Complete set lists for $85.

1985: A Father & Son Feature (131-143) is again included . . . Set features rookie cards of Scott Bankhead (393), Mike Dunne (395), Shane Mack (398), John Marzano (399), Oddibe McDowell (400), Mark McGwire (401), Pat Pacillo (402), Cory Snyder (403) and Billy Swift (404) as part of salute to 1984 USA Baseball Team (389-404) that participated in Olympic Games plus rookie cards of Roger Clemens (181) and Eric Davis (627) . . . Card of McGwire lists for $20 . . . Card of Davis lists for $18 . . . Card of Clemens lists for $11 . . . Complete set lists for $95.

1986: Set includes Pete Rose Feature (2-7), which reproduces each of Rose's TOPPS cards from 1963 thru 1985 (four per card) . . . Bob Rodgers (141) should have been numbered 171 . . . Ryne Sandberg (690) is the only card with TOPPS logo omitted . . . Complete set lists for $24.

1987: Record Breakers (1-7) feature Roger Clemens, Jim Deshaies, Dwight Evans, Davey Lopes, Dave Righetti, Ruben Sierra and Todd Worrell . . . Jim Gantner (108) is shown with Brewers logo reversed . . . Complete set lists for $22.

1988: Record Breakers (1-7) include Vince Coleman, Don Mattingly, Mark McGwire, Eddie Murray, Phil & Joe Niekro, Nolan Ryan and Benny Santiago. Al Leiter (18) was originally shown with photo of minor leaguer Steve George and later corrected. Complete set lists for $20.00.

Pitching Record & Index

PLAYER	G	IP	W	L	R	ER	SO	BB	GS	CG	SHO	SV	ERA
AASE, DON	325	956.2	61	54	428	398	552	371	91	22	0	75	3.74
ALLEN, LLOYD	159	297	8	25			194	196	19	2	0	22	4.70
BAHNSEN, STAN	574	2527	146	149			1359	924	327	73	16	20	3.61
BARBER, STEVE	466	1998	121	106			1309	950	272	59	21	13	3.36
BARLOW, MIKE	133	247	10	6			96	104	2	0	0	6	4.63
BARR, JIM	454	2064.1	101	112			741	469	252	64	20	12	3.56
BELINSKY, BO	146	665	28	51			476	323	102	14	6	2	4.10
BENNETT, DENNIS	182	863	43	47			572	281	127	28	6	2	3.69
BLATERIC, STEVE	5	11	0	0			13	1	0	0	0	0	5.73
BORBON, PEDRO	593	1026	69	39			409	251	4	0	0	80	3.52
BOTTING, RALPH	18	56	2	3			34	28	7	0	0	0	7.39
BOWSFIELD, TED	215	663	37	39			326	259	86	12	2	6	4.34
BRADLEY, TOM	183	1018	55	61			691	311	151	27	10	6	3.72
BRETT, KEN	349	1526	83	85			807	562	184	51	8	11	3.93
BREWER, JIM	584	1044	69	65			810	360	35	1	1	132	3.06
BRUNET, GEORGE	324	1431	69	93			921	581	213	39	15	4	3.62
BRYDEN, T.R.	16	34.1	2	1	25	25	25	21	0	0	0	0	6.55
BURDETTE, LEW	626	3068	203	144			1074	628	373	158	33	31	3.66
BURGMEIER, TOM	745	1258.1	79	55			584	384	3	0	0	102	3.23
CANDELARIA, JOHN	350	2016.2	141	89	775	698	1276	477	300	47	11	15	3.12
CASALE, JERRY	96	371	17	24			207	234	49	10	3	2	5.07
CHANCE, DEAN	406	2148	128	115			1534	739	294	83	33	23	2.92
CIMINO, PETE	86	161	5	8			139	65	4	1	1	5	3.07
CLARK, RICKEY	96	432	19	22			236	213	70	4	2	5	3.38
CLEAR, MARK	394	689.1	62	44			691	469	0	0	0	77	3.80
CLEMENTS, PAT	133	157.1	5	6			67	72	0	0	0	5	3.20
CLEVENGER, TEX	307	696	36	37			361	298	40	6	0	30	4.18
CLIBURN, STU	45	101	9	3			49	27	0	0	0	6	2.32
COATES, JIM	247	683	43	22			396	286	46	13	0	18	4.01
CORBETT, DOUG	302	530	24	28	206	184	327	187	1	0	0	65	3.12
COX, TERRY	3	18.2	1	0			12	10	4	0	0	0	4.27
CUELLAR, MIKE	453	2807	185	130			1632	822	379	172	36	11	3.14
CUMBERLAND, JOHN	110	335	15	16			137	103	36	6	2	2	3.81
CURTIS, JOHN	438	1641	89	97			825	669	199	42	14	1	3.96
D'ACQUISTO, JOHN	266	780	34	51			600	544	92	7	2	15	4.56
DOBSON, CHUCK	202	1258	74	69			758	476	190	49	11	0	3.78
DONOHUE, JIM	70	156	9	4			116	82	9	0	0	7	4.27
DORSEY, JIM	9	18.2	1	2			12	11	4	0	0	0	9.16
DOYLE, PAUL	87	90	5	3			65	46	0	0	0	11	3.80
DRAGO, DICK	519	1876	108	117			987	558	189	62	10	58	3.62
DUKES, TOM	161	217	5	16			169	82	0	0	0	21	4.35
DULIBA, BOB	176	258	17	12			129	96	0	0	0	14	3.45
DUNNING, STEVE	134	612	23	41			390	323	84	7	1	1	4.57
DUREN, RYNE	311	590	27	44			630	392	32	2	1	57	3.83
EGAN, DICK	74	101	1	2			68	41	0	0	0	2	5.17
ELLIS, SAMMY	229	1004	63	58			677	378	140	35	9	18	4.15
FIGUEROA, ED	200	1310	80	68			571	443	179	63	12	0	3.51
FINLEY, CHUCK	25	46.1	3	1	17	17	37	23	0	0	0	0	3.30
FISHER, EDDIE	690	1541	85	70			812	438	63	7	2	81	3.40
FITZMORRIS, AL	288	1277	77	59			458	164	241	36	9	7	3.65
FORSCH, KEN	512	2108.2	114	112			1034	576	241	70	18	50	3.32
FORSTER, TERRY	614	1105.1	54	65	454	397	791	457	39	5	0	127	3.23
FOSTER, ALAN	217	1028	48	63			501	383	148	26	5	0	3.73
FOWLER, ART	362	1025	54	51			539	308	90	25	4	32	4.02
FOWLKES, ALAN	21	85	4	2			50	24	15	1	0	0	5.19
FOYTACK, PAUL	312	1499	86	87			827	662	193	63	7	7	4.14

PLAYER	G	IP	W	L	R	ER	SO	BB	GS	CG	SHO	SV	ERA
FROST, DAVE	99	549.2	33	37			222	174	84	16	3	1	4.11
GARRETT, GREG	34	84	5	7			55	54	8	0	0	3	2.46
GARVER, NED	402	2477	129	157			881	881	330	153	18	12	3.73
GATEWOOD, AUBREY	68	178	8	9			75	67	13	1	0	0	2.78
GEISHERT, VERN	11	31	1	1			18	7	3	0	0	0	4.65
GOLTZ, DAVE	353	2038.1	113	119			1105	646	264	83	13	8	3.69
GRBA, ELI	135	536	23	33			255	284	75	10	0	4	4.48
GRIFFIN, TOM	401	1493.1	77	94			1054	769	191	29	10	5	4.07
HALICKI, ED	192	1063	55	66			707	534	157	36	13	1	3.62
HAMILTON, JACK	218	612	32	40			357	238	65	8	2	20	4.53
HAND, RICH	104	488	24	39			278	250	78	6	1	3	4.00
HARRELSON, BILL	10	34	1	6			22	26	5	0	0	0	5.03
HARTZELL, PAUL	170	703.1	27	39			237	181	87	22	2	12	3.90
HASSLER, ANDY	377	1113	44	70			625	516	112	26	5	29	3.85
HEFFNER, BOB	114	354	11	21			241	107	31	4	2	6	4.50
HEMAN, RUS	12	20	0	0			6	10	1	0	0	0	2.70
HOLLAND, AL	356	598.2	33	30			471	214	10	0	0	78	2.72
JAMES, JOHNNY	66	119	5	3			73	84	3	0	0	2	4.76
JEFFERSON, JESSE	237	1086	39	81			522	520	144	25	4	4	4.81
JOHN, TOMMY	684	4279.2	264	210	1781	1536	2083	1144	625	159	45	4	3.23
KAUFMAN, CURT	40	86.1	3	5			50	30	1	0	0	1	4.48
KEALEY, STEVE	139	214	9	8			126	69	4	1	1	11	4.29
KELSO, BILL	119	201	12	5			162	93	2	0	0	12	3.13
KIPPER, BOB	27	142	7	11			94	44	24	0	0	0	4.63
KIRKWOOD, DON	120	375	18	23			194	135	37	7	0	8	4.37
KISON, BRUCE	380	1809	115	88			1073	662	246	36	8	12	3.66
KLINE, RON	736	2078	114	144			989	731	203	44	8	108	3.86
KNAPP, CHRIS	122	603	36	32			355	250	99	15	0	0	5.00
KUHAULUA, FRED	8	35	1	0			19	16	5	0	0	0	4.89
LA ROCHE, DAVE	647	1049	65	58			819	459	15	1	0	126	3.53
LACEY, BOB	284	451.2	20	29			251	139	22	2	1	22	3.67
LACORTE, FRANK	253	490	23	44			372	258	32	3	0	26	5.01
LANGE, DICK	70	277	9	15			137	123	31	3	0	1	4.45
LASHER, FRED	151	202	11	13			148	110	1	0	0	22	3.88
LATMAN, BARRY	344	1219	59	68			829	489	134	28	10	16	3.91
LAZORKO, JACK	15	39.2	0	1			24	22	7	0	0	1	4.31
LEE, BOB	269	492	25	23			315	196	7	0	0	63	2.71
LEE, DON	244	828	40	44			467	281	97	13	4	11	3.61
LEE, MIKE	13	35	1	1			17	25	0	0	0	0	3.34
LEMANCZYK, DAVE	185	912	37	63			429	363	103	30	3	0	4.63
LOCKE, BOBBY	165	416	16	15			194	165	23	2	0	10	4.02
LOCKWOOD, SKIP	420	1236	57	97			829	490	106	16	5	68	3.55
LOPEZ, MARCELINO	171	653	31	40			426	317	93	40	3	2	3.62
LUCAS, GARY	361	594.1	28	39			366	192	18	0	0	60	2.94
LUGO, URBANO	26	104.1	4	5			51	35	13	1	0	0	3.71
MAHLER, MICKEY	122	406	14	32			262	190	58	3	1	4	4.68
MALONEY, JIM	301	1849	134	84			1605	810	262	74	30	4	3.19
MARTINEZ, FRED	32	155	7	9			62	23	23	4	1	0	4.47
MAY, RUDY	535	2621.1	152	156			1760	958	360	87	24	12	3.46
MCBRIDE, KEN	151	808	40	50			503	353	122	28	7	3	3.79
MCCASKILL, KIRK	64	436	29	22			156	62	62	16	3	0	3.94
MCGLOTHLIN, JIM	256	1300	67	77			544	418	201	36	8	2	3.61
MCLOUGHLIN, BYRON	129	378.2	16	25			248	171	35	5	0	16	5.11
MESSERSMITH, ANDY	344	2230	130	99			1625	831	296	103	27	15	2.86
MEYER, BOB	38	129	2	12			92	80	18	3	0	0	4.40
MILLER, DYAR	251	466	23	17			235	177	1	0	0	3	3.23

PLAYER	G	IP	W	L	R	ER	SO	BB	GS	CG	SHO	SV	ERA
MINTON, GREG	537	847.1	44	52	352	303	343	366	7	0	0	124	3.22
MOELLER, RON	52	153	6	9			104	100	22	1	1	0	5.76
MONGE, SID	435	764.1	49	40			471	356	17	4	0	56	3.53
MONTAGUE, JOHN	223	548	24	26			260	226	17	2	0	21	4.75
MONTEAGUDO, AURELIO	75	131	3	7			58	62	7	0	0	4	5.08
MOORE, BALOR	180	719	28	48			496	365	98	16	4	1	4.52
MOORE, DONNIE	375	596.1	36	36	276	241	377	165	4	0	0	80	3.64
MORGAN, TOM	443	1025	67	47			364	300	61	18	7	64	3.60
MURPHY, TOM	439	1443	68	101			621	493	147	22	2	59	3.78
NAVARRO, JULIO	130	211	7	9			151	70	1	0	0	17	3.67
NELSON, MEL	93	174	4	10			98	69	11	1	0	5	4.40
NEWMAN, FRED	108	610	33	39			254	154	93	18	4	0	3.41
NOLAN, GARY	250	1675	110	70			1039	413	247	45	14	0	3.08
NUXHALL, JOE	526	2304	135	117			1372	776	287	83	20	19	3.90
ORTEGA, PHIL	204	952	46	62			549	378	141	20	5	2	4.42
OSINKSI, DAN	324	590	29	28			400	264	21	5	2	18	2.34
OVERY, MIKE	5	7	0	2			8	8	3	0	0	0	6.43
PACTWA, JOE	4	16	0	0			3	10	0	0	0	0	3.94
PATTIN, MARTY	475	2038	114	109			1179	603	224	64	14	25	3.62
PENA, ORLANDO	427	1203	56	77			818	352	93	21	4	40	3.70
PERRANOSKI, RON	737	1176	79	74			687	468	1	0	0	179	2.79
PHILLIPS, LEFTY	No major league statistics												
PICHE, RON	134	221	10	16			157	123	11	3	0	12	4.19
PINA, HORACIO	314	432	23	23			278	216	7	0	0	38	3.25
PRIDDY, BOB	249	535	24	38			294	198	29	3	0	18	4.00
RAU, DOUG	222	1261	81	60			697	382	187	33	11	3	3.35
REED, HOWIE	229	516	26	29			268	208	35	3	1	9	3.72
RENKO, STEVE	451	2493.	134	146			1455	1010	365	57	9	6	4.00
REUSS, JERRY	537	3218.2	194	163	1438	1251	1744	1018	468	123	37	11	3.50
REYNOLDS, ARCHIE	36	81	0	8			47	49	7	0	0	0	5.78
ROGAN, PAT	No major league statistics												
ROJAS, MINNIE	157	261	23	16			153	66	2	0	0	43	3.00
ROMANICK, RON	82	531	31	29	276	250	189	167	82	15	4	0	4.24
ROSE, DON	19	46	1	4			40	20	4	0	0	0	4.11
ROSS, GARY	283	713	25	47			378	288	49	8	2	7	3.92
RUHLE, VERN	327	1410.2	67	88	675	585	582	348	188	29	12	11	3.73
RYAN, NOLAN	611	4115.1	253	226	1643	1440	4277	2268	577	203	54	3	3.15
SANCHEZ, LUIS	194	370	28	21			216	145	1	0	0	27	3.75
SANDERS, KEN	408	657	29	45			360	258	1	0	0	86	2.97
SANFORD, JACK	388	2047	137	101			1182	737	293	76	14	11	3.69
SCOTT, MICKEY	133	172	8	7			70	50	0	0	0	4	3.71
SELLS, DAVE	90	130	11	7			49	67	0	0	0	12	3.91
SELMA, DICK	307	841	42	54			681	381	76	11	6	31	3.62
SEMPROCH, RAY	85	344	19	21			156	136	48	14	2	3	4.42
SIMMONS, CURT	569	3349	193	183			1697	1063	461	163	36	5	3.54
SIMPSON, WAYNE	122	636	36	31			353	315	107	13	2	5	4.37
SINGER, BILL	322	2174	118	127			1515	781	308	96	24	2	3.39
SLATON, JIM	496	2683.2	151	158	1335	1202	1191	1004	360	86	22	14	4.03
SPRING, JACK	155	186	12	5			86	78	5	0	0	8	4.26
STONEMAN, BILL	245	1238	54	84			934	602	170	46	15	5	4.08
SUKLA, ED	39	52	3	5			26	17	0	0	0	4	5.19
SUTTON, DON	723	5002.2	310	239	1959	1776	3431	1272	706	177	58	5	3.20
SWAN, CRAIG	231	1234.1	59	72			673	368	185	25	7	2	3.75
TANANA, FRANK	408	2758.1	159	153	1180	1041	1925	772	392	123	28	0	3.40
TATUM, KEN	176	283	16	12			156	117	2	0	0	52	2.93
TIANT, LUIS	573	3485.2	229	172			2416	1104	484	187	49	15	3.30
TRAVERS, BILL	205	1120.2	65	71			488	415	168	46	10	1	4.10
TURLEY, BOB	310	1711	101	85			1265	1068	237	78	24	12	3.65
VERHOEVEN, JOHN	99	204	3	8			90	63	0	0	0	4	3.79

PLAYER	G	IP	W	L	R	ER	SO	BB	GS	CG	SHO	SV	ERA
WASHBURN, GREG	8	11	0	2			4	1	7	0	0	0	8.18
WEAVER, JIM	27	53	3	1			28	19	2	1	0	1	2.55
WHEELOCK, GARY	20	93	6	9			50	28	18	2	0	0	5.42
WILHELM, HOYT	1070	2253	143	122			1610	778	52	20	5	227	2.52
WILLHITE, NICK	58	182	6	12			118	75	29	3	1	1	4.55
WITT, GEORGE	66	229	11	16			156	127	38	5	3	0	4.32
WITT, MIKE	201	1228.1	71	59	540	480	821	424	169	43	8	5	3.52
WOLF, WALLY	6	7	0	0			7	7	0	0	0	0	7.71
WRIGHT, CLYDE	329	1729	100	111			667	550	235	67	9	3	3.50
WYNNE, BILLY	42	188	8	11			97	78	30	6	1	0	4.31
ZAHN, GEOFF	304	1848.2	111	109			705	526	270	79	20	1	3.74

Batting Record & Index

PLAYER	G	AB	R	H	2B	3B	HR	RBI	SB	SLG	BB	SO	AVG
ADAMS, RICKY	120	247	35	53	5	1	4	16	2	.291	11	37	.215
ADCOCK, JOE	1959	6606	823	1832	295	35	336	1122	20	.485	594	1059	.277
AIKENS, WILLIE	762	2472	299	671	124	2	109	410	3	.456	317	438	.271
ALLIETTA, BOB	21	45	4	8	1	0	1	6	0	.267	17	6	.178
ALOMAR, SANDY	1481	4760	558	1168	126	19	13	282	227	.288	302	482	.245
AMARO, RUBEN	940	2155	211	505	75	13	8	156	11	.292	227	280	.234
ANDERSON, JIM	419	970	107	249	35	2	13	86	9	.285	130	130	.218
ARMAS, TONY	1224	4513	542	1134	174	35	224	727	16	.454	230	1055	.251
ASPROMONTE, KEN	475	1483	171	369	69	3	19	124	7	.338	179	149	.249
AVERILL, EARL	449	1031	137	249	41	0	44	159	2	.409	162	220	.242
AZCUE, JOE	909	2828	201	712	94	9	50	304	5	.344	207	344	.252
BAILEY, ED	1212	3583	432	915	128	15	155	540	17	.429	545	577	.256
BALAZ, JOHN	59	162	14	39	8	1	7	15	0	.340	21	35	.241
BAYLOR, DON	2072	7546	1141	1982	350	28	315	1179	280	.442	726	966	.263
BECQUER, JULIO	488	974	100	238	36	16	12	114	8	.352	45	120	.244
BENIQUEZ, JUAN	1377	4338	581	1193	176	29	70	421	104	.377	325	507	.275
BERRY, KEN	1383	4156	422	1053	150	23	58	343	45	.342	298	569	.253
BILKO, STEVE	600	1738	220	432	85	13	76	276	2	.444	234	395	.249
BOCHTE, BRUCE	1538	5233	643	1478	250	21	100	658	43	.396	653	662	.282
BONDS, BOBBY	1849	7043	1258	1886	302	66	332	1024	461	.471	914	1757	.268
BOONE, BOB	1843	5982	557	1501	252	24	96	702	32	.349	533	497	.251
BOSLEY, THAD	587	1276	152	353	37	11	17	121	43	.363	119	213	.277
BOSTOCK, LYMAN	526	2004	305	624	102	30	23	250	45	.427	171	174	.311
BRICKELL, FRITZ	41	88	7	16	1	0	1	7	0	.227	19	19	.182
BRIDGES, ROCKY	919	2272	245	562	80	11	16	187	10	.313	205	229	.247
BRIGGS, DAN	325	688	67	134	20	6	12	53	2	.294	45	133	.195
BROOKS, BOBBY	55	143	19	23	3	0	5	20	0	.378	29	42	.231
BROWN, MIKE	297	853	101	228	47	7	23	110	2	.420	76	123	.267
BRUNANSKY, TOM	758	2765	369	687	131	11	133	384	25	.448	302	484	.248
BUCKNER, BILL	2176	8424	1008	2464	464	46	164	1007	175	.417	402	395	.292
BURKE, LEO	165	301	33	72	7	2	9	45	2	.365	21	79	.239
BURLESON, RICK	1284	4933	630	1358	242	22	48	435	72	.362	403	447	.275
CAMPANERIS, BERT	2327	8684	1181	2249	313	86	79	646	649	.342	618	1142	.259
CARDENAS, JOSE	2017	6964	936	1913	333	46	118	775	329	.395	608	807	.275
CARDENAS, LEO	1941	6705	662	1725	285	49	118	689	39	.367	522	1135	.257
CAREW, ROD	2469	9315	1424	3053	445	112	92	1015	353	.429	1018	1028	.328
CAUSEY, WAYNE	1105	3244	357	819	130	26	35	295	12	.341	390	341	.252
CERV, BOB	829	2261	320	624	96	26	105	374	12	.481	212	392	.276
CHALK, DAVE	903	2910	292	733	107	9	15	243	36	.310	295	327	.252
CHANCE, BOB	277	747	76	195	34	1	24	112	0	.406	68	195	.261
CIMOLI, GINO	969	3054	370	808	133	48	44	321	21	.383	221	474	.265
CLARK, BOB	396	967	97	231	34	7	19	100	4	.347	55	199	.239
CLINTON, LU	691	2153	270	532	112	31	65	269	22	.418	188	418	.247
COLLINS, DAVE	1368	4484	612	1231	150	50	32	344	369	.356	442	594	.275
CONIGLIARO, TONY	876	3221	464	849	139	23	166	516	20	.476	287	629	.264
CONSOLO, BILLY	603	1178	158	260	37	11	9	83	5	.289	297	297	.221
COTTIER, CHUCK	580	1584	168	348	63	17	19	127	28	.317	137	248	.220
COUGHTRY, MARLAN	35	54	5	10	1	0	0	4	0	.185	13	18	.185
COWAN, BILLY	493	1190	131	281	44	8	40	125	17	.387	50	297	.236
COWENS, AL	1556	5452	699	1479	272	68	108	711	119	.406	386	641	.271
CRUZ, TODD	544	1526	133	336	58	6	34	154	10	.333	55	318	.220
DADE, PAUL	439	1313	186	355	54	7	10	107	57	.345	113	193	.270
DAVALILLO, VIC	1458	4017	509	1122	160	37	36	329	123	.364	212	422	.279
DAVANON, JERRY	262	499	73	117	19	3	6	50	3	.315	48	80	.234
DAVIS, BOB J.E.	290	665	50	131	21	5	9	51	0	.262	40	118	.197
DAVIS, TOMMY	1999	7223	811	2121	272	35	153	1052	136	.405	381	754	.294

PLAYER	G	AB	R	H	2B	3B	HR	RBI	SB	SLG	BB	SO	AVG
DAVIS, WILLIE	2429	9174	1217	2561	395	138	182	1053	397	.412	408	977	.279
DECINCES, DOUG	1512	5347	712	1397	287	29	221	815	55	.450	548	815	.261
DEES, CHARLIE	98	260	27	69	12	1	4	29	5	.354	13	43	.265
DOHERTY, JOHN	104	317	27	76	17	1	1	27	3	.338	16	25	.240
DONOHUE, TOM	122	325	31	65	7	2	5	28	7	.280	10	92	.200
DOWNING, BRIAN	1586	5201	763	1382	235	17	166	734	40	.413	784	719	.266
DOYLE, DENNY	944	3290	357	823	113	28	16	237	38	.316	205	310	.250
EASLER, MIKE	1053	3400	445	1000	179	25	113	491	19	.461	301	644	.294
EGAN, TOM	373	979	74	196	25	3	22	91	2	.299	80	336	.200
ELLIOTT, RANDY	114	288	31	62	12	2	8	35	0	.354	18	57	.215
EPSTEIN, MIKE	907	2854	362	695	93	4	130	380	7	.424	448	645	.244
ETCHEBARREN, ANDY	948	2618	245	615	101	17	49	309	13	.343	246	529	.235
FAIRLY, RON	2442	7184	931	1913	307	33	215	1044	35	.408	1052	877	.266
FERGUSON, JOE	1013	2951	407	719	121	11	122	445	22	.416	565	607	.244
FIMPLE, JACK	66	174	18	42	12	1	2	25	1	.399	12	45	.241
FLORES, GIL	185	464	58	121	20	6	2	37	15	.343	34	61	.261
FOILES, HANK	608	1455	171	353	59	10	46	166	3	.392	170	295	.243
FOLI, TIM	1677	6010	575	1508	241	20	25	499	81	.310	295	397	.251
FORD, DAN	1153	4163	598	1123	214	38	121	566	61	.427	303	722	.270
FREGOSI, JIM	1902	6523	844	1726	264	78	151	706	76	.398	715	1097	.265
GABRIELSON, LEN	708	1764	178	446	64	12	37	176	20	.366	145	315	.253
GALLAGHER, ALAN	442	1264	114	333	42	9	11	130	7	.337	138	164	.263
GARCIA, DAVE	No major league statistics												
GARR, RALPH	1317	5108	717	1562	212	64	75	408	172	.416	246	445	.306
GARRETT, ADRIAN	163	276	30	51	8	1	11	37	4	.333	31	87	.185
GERBER, CRAIG	65	91	8	24	1	2	0	3	0	.319	3	3	.264
GONZALEZ, TONY	1559	5195	690	1485	238	57	103	615	79	.413	467	706	.286
GOODWIN, DANNY	252	636	72	150	32	3	13	81	3	.373	61	137	.236
GOTAY, JULIO	389	988	106	257	41	8	6	70	12	.323	61	127	.260
GRABARKEWITZ, BILLY	466	1161	189	274	48	12	28	141	33	.364	202	321	.236
GREEN, LENNY	1136	2956	461	788	138	27	47	253	78	.379	368	260	.267
GRICH, BOB	2008	6890	1033	1833	320	47	224	864	104	.424	1087	1278	.266
GRIFFIN, DOUG	632	2136	209	524	70	12	7	165	33	.299	158	204	.245
GUERRERO, MARIO	697	2251	167	578	79	12	8	170	8	.312	84	152	.257
HALL, JIMMIE	968	2848	387	724	100	24	121	391	38	.434	287	529	.254
HAMLIN, KEN	468	1340	143	323	53	4	11	89	17	.311	125	146	.241
HAMPTON, IKE	113	135	15	28	4	1	4	18	1	.341	11	38	.207
HARLOW, LARRY	449	1094	159	271	48	8	12	72	26	.339	156	205	.248
HARPER, BRIAN	175	337	30	82	13	1	11	44	1	.386	10	34	.243
HARPER, TOMMY	1810	6269	972	1609	256	36	146	567	408	.379	753	1080	.257
HARRIS, JOHN	56	120	13	31	8	0	1	16	0	.450	10	15	.258
HEISE, BOBBY	499	1144	104	283	43	3	1	86	3	.293	47	77	.247
HELD, WOODY	1390	4019	524	963	150	22	179	559	14	.421	509	944	.240
HENDRICK, GEORGE	1914	6840	915	1910	332	27	259	1067	59	.449	546	975	.279
HERNANDEZ, JACKIE	618	1480	153	308	37	9	10	121	25	.270	93	324	.208
HERRMANN, ED	922	2729	247	654	95	5	80	320	6	.364	260	361	.240
HIATT, JACK	483	1142	110	287	51	5	22	154	0	.363	224	295	.251
HICKS, JIM	93	141	16	23	1	3	5	14	0	.319	14	48	.163
HINTON, CHUCK	1353	3968	518	1048	152	47	113	443	130	.412	416	685	.264
HOBSON, BUTCH	738	2556	314	634	107	23	98	397	11	.423	183	569	.248
HOWELL, JACK	106	288	45	68	18	2	6	39	5	.406	35	61	.236
HUMPHREY, TERRY	415	1055	69	223	39	1	6	85	5	.267	68	175	.211
HUNT, KEN L.	310	782	107	177	42	4	33	111	9	.417	85	222	.226
JACKSON, REGGIE	2705	9528	1509	2510	449	48	548	1659	226	.493	1342	2500	.263
JACKSON, RON	926	2986	356	774	165	22	78	342	18	.385	213	329	.259
JOHNSON, ALEX	1322	4623	550	1331	180	33	78	525	103	.392	244	626	.288

PLAYER	G	AB	R	H	2B	3B	HR	RBI	SB	SLG	BB	SO	AVG
JOHNSON, LOU	677	2049	244	529	97	14	48	232	50	.389	110	320	.258
JOHNSTONE, JAY	1748	4703	578	1254	215	38	102	531	50	.394	429	632	.267
JONES, BOB	301	582	64	131	17	0	20	83	18	.357	48	112	.225
JONES, RUPPERT	1246	4223	618	1056	207	36	139	551	141	.415	514	779	.250
JOYNER, WALLY	154	593	82	172	27	3	22	100	5	.457	57	58	.290
KELLEHER, MICK	622	1081	108	230	32	6	0	65	8	.253	74	133	.213
KINGMAN, DAVE	1941	6677	901	1575	240	25	442	1210	85	.478	608	1816	.236
KIRKPATRICK, ED	1311	3467	411	824	143	18	85	425	34	.363	456	518	.238
KLUSZEWSKI, TED	1718	5929	848	1766	290	29	279	1028	20	.498	492	365	.298
KNOOP, BOBBY	1153	3622	337	856	129	29	56	331	16	.334	305	623	.236
KOPPE, JOE	578	1606	202	379	61	12	19	141	5	.324	209	345	.236
KOSCO, ANDY	658	1963	204	464	75	5	73	267	5	.394	99	350	.236
KOSTRO, FRANK	266	467	40	114	17	1	5	37	1	.321	33	61	.244
KUSNYER, ART	139	313	21	55	6	1	5	37	0	.230	38	61	.176
LAHOUD, JOE	791	1925	239	429	68	12	65	218	20	.372	309	339	.223
LANDREAUX, KEN	1149	3919	505	1062	176	45	85	456	140	.404	283	393	.271
LANSFORD, CARNEY	1139	4478	634	1307	212	30	113	563	108	.428	319	524	.292
LEEK, GENE	77	249	23	55	12	0	6	25	0	.349	23	67	.221
LEJA, FRANK	26	23	3	1	0	0	0	0	0	.043	1	8	.043
LINARES, RUFINO	189	502	59	136	19	3	8	52	13	.369	21	69	.271
LLENAS, WINSTON	300	531	50	122	17	1	8	61	2	.279	38	69	.230
LOPEZ, CARLOS	237	500	61	130	24	1	12	54	23	.384	25	98	.260
LUBRATICH, STEVE	64	177	14	37	1	0	0	8	1	.266	19	19	.209
LYNN, FRED	1537	5589	906	1632	336	40	241	926	64	.496	716	847	.292
MALZONE, FRANK	1441	5428	647	1486	239	21	133	728	14	.399	337	434	.274
MAUCH, GENE	304	737	93	176	25	7	5	62	6	.312	104	82	.239
MAY, CARLOS	1165	4120	544	1127	172	23	90	536	85	.392	512	544	.274
McCRAW, TOM	1468	3956	484	972	150	42	75	404	143	.362	332	544	.246
McFARLANE, ORLANDO	124	292	22	70	12	0	5	20	0	.332	20	93	.240
McMULLEN, KEN	1583	5131	568	1273	172	26	156	606	20	.383	510	815	.248
McNAMARA, JOHN	No major league statistics												
MELTON, BILL	1144	3972	499	1004	162	4	160	591	23	.419	479	669	.253
MEOLI, RUDY	310	626	69	133	20	4	4	40	10	.267	69	88	.212
MILEY, MIKE	84	262	21	46	5	2	2	12	1	.256	20	62	.176
MILLER, DARRELL	101	146	19	38	4	0	2	30	0	.356	9	27	.260
MILLER, RICK	1482	3887	552	1046	161	35	28	369	78	.350	454	583	.269
MINCHER, DON	1400	4026	530	1003	176	16	200	643	24	.450	668	668	.249
MONTANEZ, WILLIE	1632	5843	645	1604	279	25	139	802	32	.402	465	751	.275
MORAN, BILLY	634	2076	242	545	88	10	28	202	10	.355	133	218	.263
MORTON, BUBBA	451	928	117	248	37	8	14	128	14	.370	111	143	.267
MOSES, GERRY	385	1072	89	269	48	8	25	109	1	.381	63	184	.251
MOTTON, CURT	316	567	85	121	21	2	25	89	5	.384	86	116	.213
MULLINKS, RANCE	822	2288	295	614	150	12	43	273	11	.401	269	340	.268
NARRON, JERRY	388	832	64	177	23	0	21	96	1	.321	67	125	.213
NETTLES, MORRIS	168	469	77	116	15	1	0	31	42	.279	43	95	.247
NORDBROOK, TIM	128	169	27	30	2	1	1	3	2	.195	25	26	.178
O'BERRY, MIKE	177	355	36	68	10	1	2	28	0	.251	30	74	.192
O'BRIEN, SYD	378	1052	135	242	35	8	24	100	5	.347	60	155	.230
OLIVER, BOB	847	2914	293	745	102	19	94	419	17	.400	156	562	.256
OTT, ED	567	1792	196	465	76	10	33	195	14	.368	138	254	.259
OYLER, RAY	542	1265	110	221	39	6	15	86	2	.251	135	359	.175
PARKER, BILLY	94	252	29	56	4	2	3	21	5	.290	19	60	.222
PATEK, FREDDIE	1650	5530	736	1340	216	55	41	490	385	.324	523	787	.242
PEARSON, ALBIE	988	3077	485	831	130	24	28	214	77	.355	477	195	.270
PEREZ, MARTY	931	3131	313	771	108	22	22	241	11	.316	245	369	.246
PERRY, BOB	131	387	35	103	18	1	6	30	1	.362	23	83	.266
PETTIS, GARY	567	1469	247	369	46	21	12	126	162	.336	198	562	.251
PICCIOLO, ROB	451	1469	192	381	56	10	17	109	9	.312	25	254	.234
PIERSALL, JIMMY	1734	5890	811	1604	256	52	104	591	115	.386	583	583	.272

PLAYER	G	AB	R	H	2B	3B	HR	RBI	SB	SLG	BB	SO	AVG
QUEEN, MEL	269	274	20	49	7	1	2	25	0	.226	21	50	.179
RAMIREZ, ORLANDO	143	281	24	53	5	1	0	16	16	.214	24	65	.189
RANEW, MERRITT	269	594	68	147	18	9	8	54	3	.352	42	120	.247
RAY, JOHNNY	808	3053	366	880	183	23	32	327	64	.395	218	171	.288
REICHARDT, RICK	997	3307	391	864	109	24	116	445	40	.414	263	672	.261
REMY, JERRY	1154	4455	605	1226	140	38	7	329	208	.328	356	404	.275
REPOZ, ROGER	831	2145	257	480	73	19	82	260	26	.390	499	499	.224
RETTENMUND, MERV	1023	2555	393	693	114	16	66	329	68	.406	445	382	.271
REYNOLDS, TOMMIE	513	1170	141	265	35	12	12	87	12	.296	166	222	.226
RICE, DEL	1309	3826	342	908	177	20	79	441	2	.356	382	522	.237
RIGNEY, BILL	654	1966	281	510	78	14	41	212	25	.376	266	206	.259
RIVERS, MICKEY	1467	5629	785	1660	247	71	61	499	267	.397	266	471	.295
ROBINSON, FRANK	2808	10006	1829	2943	528	72	586	1812	204	.537	1420	1532	.294
RODGERS, BOB	932	3033	259	704	114	18	31	288	17	.312	234	409	.232
RODRIGUEZ, AURELIO	2017	6611	612	1570	287	46	124	648	35	.351	324	943	.237
RODRIGUEZ, ELLIE	857	2173	220	533	76	6	16	203	17	.308	332	291	.245
ROOF, PHIL	857	2151	190	463	69	13	43	210	11	.319	184	504	.215
RUDI, JOE	1547	5556	684	1468	287	39	179	810	25	.427	369	851	.264
RUIZ, CHICO	565	1150	133	276	37	10	2	69	34	.295	58	164	.240
SADOWSKI, BOB F.	184	329	38	73	19	3	7	46	5	.331	63	63	.222
SADOWSKI, ED	217	495	55	100	20	1	12	39	1	.319	39	94	.202
SANDS, CHARLIE	93	145	15	31	6	1	6	23	0	.393	35	35	.214
SATRIANO, TOM	674	1623	130	365	53	5	21	157	7	.303	214	225	.225
SCHAAL, PAUL	1128	3555	436	869	132	26	57	323	43	.344	516	466	.244
SCHEINBLUM, RICHIE	462	1218	131	320	52	9	13	127	9	.352	149	135	.263
SCHOFIELD, DICK	447	1350	160	298	48	12	28	123	39	.356	122	212	.221
SCONIERS, DARYL	234	637	83	169	30	3	15	84	7	.399	48	87	.265
SHOCKLEY, COSTEN	51	142	9	28	5	0	3	19	0	.275	11	24	.197
SIEBERN, NORM	1406	4481	662	1217	206	38	132	636	18	.423	708	749	.272
SILVERIO, TOM	31	30	9	3	0	0	0	0	2	.100	2	9	.100
SIMPSON, DICK	288	518	94	107	19	2	15	56	10	.338	64	174	.207
SKAGGS, DAVE	205	510	44	123	18	2	3	49	0	.302	51	76	.241
SKOWRON, BILL	1658	5547	681	1566	243	53	211	888	16	.459	383	870	.282
SLATER, BOB	No major league statistics												
SMITH, BILLY E.	370	1018	107	234	38	5	17	111	8	.335	96	189	.230
SMITH, BOBBY GENE	476	962	101	234	35	13	13	96	5	.331	55	154	.243
SMITH, WILLIE	691	1654	171	410	63	21	46	211	20	.395	107	284	.248
SOLAITA, TONY	525	1316	164	336	66	1	50	203	2	.421	234	255	.255
SPANGLER, AL	912	2267	307	594	87	26	21	175	37	.351	295	234	.262
SPENCER, JIM	1553	4908	541	1227	179	27	146	599	11	.387	407	593	.250
STANTON, LEROY	829	2575	294	628	114	13	77	358	36	.388	182	636	.244
STELMASZEK, RICK	60	88	4	15	3	0	1	10	0	.239	17	18	.170
STEPHENSON, JOHN	451	989	83	214	37	3	12	93	0	.296	63	118	.216
STUART, DICK	1112	3997	506	1055	157	30	228	743	2	.489	301	957	.264
SUDAKIS, BILL	530	1548	177	362	56	9	59	214	9	.393	169	313	.234
TANNER, CHUCK	396	885	98	231	39	5	21	105	2	.388	82	93	.261
TATUM, JARVIS	102	254	37	59	8	1	0	8	1	.264	17	50	.232
TAYLOR, BOB	394	724	56	158	25	0	16	82	5	.319	36	146	.218
THOMAS, DERREL	1597	4677	585	1163	154	54	43	370	140	.332	446	593	.249
THOMAS, GEORGE	685	1688	203	430	71	9	46	202	13	.389	138	343	.255
THOMAS, LEE	1027	3324	405	847	111	22	106	428	25	.397	397	397	.255
THOMPSON, JASON	1388	4751	634	1243	200	12	208	778	8	.440	798	850	.262
THON, DICKIE	649	2079	258	565	99	24	32	192	98	.389	162	275	.272
THRONEBERRY, FAYE	521	1302	152	307	48	12	29	137	23	.358	172	284	.236
TORBORG, JEFF	574	1391	78	297	42	3	8	101	3	.265	103	189	.214
TORRES, FELIX	365	1191	109	302	61	5	27	153	2	.381	72	202	.254
TORRES, RUSTY	654	1314	159	279	45	9	35	126	13	.334	164	246	.212
VALENTINE, BOBBY	639	1698	176	441	59	9	12	157	27	.326	140	134	.260
VALENTINE, ELLIS	883	3128	375	873	168	15	121	470	59	.458	178	454	.279